- good shindig got [...] 12-ish, went straight
[...] Sub + Met Nicol in [...]
- couple of bottles of [...]
[...] to Brighton Sunday - [...]
[...] + chips + hot doughnuts - very s[...]
[...] + back very naff design caught 17.53 train
[...] 9.20ish did kitchen floor while Bruce Irvined

[...]y.
[...] a strange mood this morning. Feeling quite long
[...]bre somehow - don't quite know what to write -
[...]ions keep floating thro' but I never have chance to
[...]em they seem to evade me - I went to get
[...] a fag + a party but I want to be left alone and
[...] cry! See I'm choking up now - should I have
[...] it's only - oh! it's later than I thought it's 11.30
[...]ay have one - it's now 12.30 went to feed
[...] ended up cleaning them out doing lamb +
[...]itchen out in general. now on my 2nd glass of wine
[...]y bit better starting to think about other things
[...] the possible bumpy path that may lay ahead.
[...]lar feel to today as most of holiday in Scotland -
[...]rong - whistling up chimney + letter box + rattling windows
[...]then sunshine. all that's needed are a few passing
[...] of venison + it'd be complete.

Time to Let Go

A Record of the Life and Death

of a

Young Man

GLOSSARY
of
medical terms used in this book

AIDS
Acquired Immune Deficiency Syndrome: AIDS itself is not an illness, but a term describing the varying collection of infections and illnesses (the 'syndrome') which result from weakening of the immune system by the virus known as HIV. The pattern varies from individual to individual. A person is not said to have AIDS until one or more of the typical infections takes hold.

AIDS-related illness
See 'Opportunistic Infections' below

AZT
Zidudovine - the principal anti-viral drug of the time, believed to inhibit the effect of HIV on the immune system. A powerful, toxic substance with potentially dangerous effects: damaging or destroying T-cells, for example, and having debilitating side-effects such as headaches and nausea.

CMV retinitis
This is one version of the CMV virus (see below) which can attack various of the body's organs and systems. This one simply destroys the retina progressively and leads to blindness.

Cryptosporidium

One of the opportunistic infections typical of AIDS. See 'Opportunistic Infections' below.

Cryptosporidium, actually untreatable, in the gut virtually destroys the body's ability to take nourishment from food or retain anything in the stomach. It also causes chronic diarrhoea. It can affect other organs too.

Cytomegalovirus (CMV)

One of the opportunistic infections typical of AIDS. See 'Opportunistic Infections' below.

CMV can affect various organs and parts of the body. Its typical activity is on the retina (where it leads to blindness) and in the gut. High-toxicity drugs like Ganciclovir and Foscarnet were thought to inhibit its progress.

Foscarnet

A high-toxicity anti-viral drug (see CMV above). Administered with additional fluid over several hours to protect the kidneys.

Ganciclovir

A high-toxicity anti-viral drug (see CMV above).

Heparin

Chemical which prevents blood clots blocking the Hickman Line.

Hickman Line

A plastic tube inserted into an artery near the heart and

protruding from the chest. Used for the direct introduction of intravenous (i/v) drugs in preference to frequent injections by needle.

HIV
Human immuno-deficiency virus: the viral infection which attacks and progressively weakens the immune system leaving the body profoundly vulnerable to 'opportunistic' and other infections. Infection occurs through direct introduction into the bloodstream from an infected person, through unprotected sex or open wounds, sharing of infected needles, or through transfusions of infected blood. There is still some controversy as to whether or not the virus can be transmitted via saliva, genital fluids or sperm.

Hyoscine
A drug used to control diarrhoea but inclined to cause hallucinations in some patients.

Kaposi's Sarcoma
A virulent skin cancer typical in the later stages of acute immune deficiency.

Midozolam
Injectable sedative like Valium, but very quick acting: excellent for distress, discomfort, agitation when the problem is not physical pain.

Opportunistic Infections

The infections typical of AIDS all result from viruses resident in the normal, healthy human body, which are suppressed by a healthy immune system. As the immune system is weakened by HIV, these viruses assert themselves and take the offered 'opportunity' to cause extensive, often terminal damage. For some of them there is no known treatment. These are collectively known as 'AIDS-related' illnesses.

A person with HIV is also, of course, much more vulnerable to the ordinary infections which can attack us all, and a simple cough or flu virus, for example, can have very serious consequences.

Palliative Care

The medical specialism concerned with the treatment of symptoms and the management of pain in chronic or terminal illness. The primary aim of palliative care is the comfort of the patient rather than the treatment and cure of disease itself.

PCP

Pneumocystis carinii pneumonia: this is one of the commonest, early opportunistic infections of a body with an immune system weakened by HIV. It causes coughing and irritation, but is amenable to treatment with Pentamadine and other drugs.

In memory of

Roy David Deakin

and in gratitude to all

who loved him and

cared for him.

Time to Let Go

A Record of the Life and Death
of a
Young Man

Bruce Hugman

Published privately in London

1999

First published in the UK 1999 Bruce Hugman
Copyright © Bruce Hugman 1999

All enquiries relating to this publication should be made to:
Bruce Hugman
34 Culverden Road
LONDON SW12 9LP
United Kingdom

Fax: +44 (0)181 675 2292
e-mail: brucehugman@compuserve.com

For availability of free and paid-for copies,
please see back of dust-jacket

Set in Bernhard Modern Roman 11pt

ISBN : 0 953453 0 6

Design and Typesetting by West Design, Buxton

Printed in England by Lakes Ltd., Birmingham

Bruce Angman (signature)

Time to Let Go

Limited Edition of

500 copies

Copy number

PREFACE

Roy Deakin died from AIDS-related illnesses on 27 March 1992 at the age of thirty-two. For nearly nine years he and I enjoyed a loving and fulfilling partnership and a rich and satisfying life. Occasionally difficult and painful, it was not always a romantic idyll, but it was constantly challenging and exciting. It took us far beyond the boundaries we should ever have crossed independently and it was far beyond anything I had ever dreamed of enjoying.

The period of his illness was, at the same time, the most beautiful and painful and intense experience of our lives. It tested our energy, our resources, our love beyond all that we could have thought possible. It was, in the event, both terrible and glorious.

This book is an account of what we made of our last two years together, and of the legacy with which I now live.

Our suffering was nothing in comparison with the many whose lives are ravaged by war or wanton killing or other sudden death. But the issues and questions and doubts and fears which we faced are the common currency of being human. How we dealt with it all, what we learnt may be of use to others, whether or not they are gay; whether or not AIDS is the threat they face.

Our good fortune was to have notice of death, and during the time of preparing ourselves to be surrounded by generous, supportive, loving friends, families and professionals. We were given much, and it was always Roy's wish - and it remains mine - to give in return when we could. I hope this book may be useful.

It was at a time when Roy was quite ill, some months before his death, that we discussed the arrangements for his funeral with the old friend who was to lead the ceremony. During that discussion, when he had so little to look forward to, he described our life together as 'a marvellous adventure'.

And so it was. I hope this account of it will touch and enrich the lives of others.

Bruce Hugman

London, November 1998

CONTENTS

PROLOGUE

The Story of a Partnership

Roy was born on 22 December 1959 to Harry and Vera Deakin. They, and his elder sister Ann, lived in a small, terraced, back-to-back house next to the River Sheaf in Sheffield. The house was lit by gas; a Yorkshire range provided the cooking facilities and the warmth for washing in the tin bath. When the Sheaf was in flood, the cellars of the whole street would be awash to ground-level.

Harry was a steam-engine fireman and then driver; Vera had been a conductress on the buses and was then was a part-time cleaning lady. Many members of the family lived in houses on the Avenue and nearby, and those others who were not related by blood were part of the tightly-knit and supportive community.

The family later moved to Rotherham and bought a house on a steep hill - far above the lapping of any potential floods.

Roy was not a great achiever at school, but, at sixteen, decided he was going to College to take 'A' levels. In his second year, Harry, just 46, died of a heart-attack.

Roy abandoned College, and started work as a bus conductor and then driver, determined to make his contribution to the household income.

Vera, in the meantime, had an operation for the removal of a benign tumour on her brain, which left her partially-sighted though physically fit. Sister Ann, by now married for some years, was bringing up her three girls fifteen miles away.

Roy was, at this time, not only hugely handsome - with neatly-trimmed full beard and moustache - but also an immensely sociable, popular man, enjoying the company of a regular group of friends with whom he went on frequent, extravagant binges. He was a smart, reliable, cheerful worker, undaunted by 4 a.m. starts or the pressures of front-line public service.

He had a very cautious, covert gay life, but shared the knowledge with only a very few friends and not at all with his mother or family. He had a few short-lived, largely unsatisfying relationships.

He was, and remained, devoted to Vera, with whom he shared a vigorous, warm-hearted satirical view of the world and human foibles and a generally earthy, suggestive sense of humour: they would often both be in helpless fits of giggles for minutes on end in response to some innuendo or ambiguity or evidence of human daftness. They both relished the peculiarities of Yorkshire folk and spoke in the rich accent and vocabulary of the region.

Vera was - and is - one of those women of heroic independence and energy who, in spite of a series of major tragedies, battles on, knowing that life continues and that time has to be filled. Losing her husband so young, facing the consequences of major surgery, discovering her son was gay and losing him to a lover, and, finally, attending the funeral of the apple of her eye when he was just thirty-two, she could have been forgiven for going into a depressive decline. But no: as ever, she continues to re-organise the house on a regular basis; to clean and decorate; to do the garden; to trim the house up for Christmas; to go out on 'biddies' trips and on holidays; to bake, cook, knit, read and write letters. She has the deep strength which comes from a fine, robust constitution, and Roy was fortunate to inherit many of those qualities.

* * * *

The circumstances of my birth and life were very different. I was the first son of Mary and Peter, a mechanical engineer and a legal secretary. Father came from the relatively liberated south while Mother came from the Presbyterian regime of the Glasgow suburbs. Both grandfathers had achieved considerable professional success as managers in business, and both had started from modest origins.

The war was to end months after my birth in January 1945, and post-war, rationed Britain formed the backcloth to my earliest memories. My brother, Iain, was born in 1949, at about the time I was sent to the first of my fee-paying schools.

In every respect, my parents did all that they could to ensure Iain and I had a good start in life. They spent endless money and trouble on wholesome food and dietary supplements (cod-liver oil capsules and Vimaltol amongst many) on dental and medical care, on schooling, on holidays at home and abroad, and on ensuring that life had occasional high-point treats such as Saturday lunch in restaurants. They were not in the least rich, but they managed their money so prudently that there was never any sign of scarcity. We had one of the earliest black and white TVs, and Dad had bought a car (a Ford Consul) just a few years after the war.

I went to a minor public school as a day-boy and then on to Oxford to get a respectable but undistinguished Second Class Honours in English Language and Literature. I stayed on for a fourth year to train as a teacher.

My career was regarded as pretty eccentric by my parents. I taught at a major public school for two years (where mother, certainly, hoped I would progress to an eventual headmastership), and then did a two-year postgraduate degree in Social Studies before becoming a probation officer. I worked on the streets of Sheffield for two years (mostly with young drug-takers and prostitutes) before moving to London as Director of the Albany, Deptford.

It was during my time in Sheffield, when I was about twenty-five, that I finally came to terms with being gay, and set out to meet other gay people and develop some kind of true and clear identity. After so many years of denial, dishonesty and mostly solitary sex, the change began to have a transforming effect on my inner confidence and available optimism, though it provoked an initially very tense time with my parents, most especially my mother.

London proved to be a difficult and painful time, and, after a year I emigrated to deepest Kent to stay with some friends in an ancient farmhouse set amidst eight acres of cherry orchards. Here, I worked for some weeks as second chef in the posh restaurant in the village and then as a general farm labourer for six months or so, seeing through lambing and harvest on our neighbour's farm.

My friends then left the house, and I and two other friends who joined me started four years of smallholding - sheep, goat, pigs, hens, ducks, a house cow, vegetables, home-made bread and all the wonderful features of the then trendy self-sufficient life. I did some adult education teaching in Canterbury and then became deputy head of English at a large secondary modern school in Whitstable.

City life eventually beckoned again, and I returned to Sheffield to a joint appointment as a training officer in the probation service and a lecturer in social studies at the Polytechnic. After four years there, I applied for the job of Public Relations Officer for South Yorkshire Transport - the huge, famous, low-fare bus operation in South Yorkshire which provoked so much national controversy for its fares policies.

It was in my second year in that job, in the summer of 1983 when I was organising our participation in the Sheffield Show, that Roy, then a bus driver in Rotherham, responded to an appeal for volunteer helpers. On a bright, sunny day, amidst milling crowds, I met him and asked him to blow up a few hundred promotional balloons for us.

He was 23, and I, 38.

* * * *

It is hard to imagine two people with apparently less cultural, social and personal compatibility than the two of us, and it is still a matter of perplexity to me what it was that made the partnership so good. In many ways we remained very distinct individuals with some very distinct tastes and habits, but a vast area of common ground was available to us, and it was on that that we discovered what we already shared and from which we took each other forward into new territories.

Within a few weeks of meeting, we spent a great deal of time together, including an idyllic long-weekend in London and Kent. We felt strongly that it would be wonderful to live in London.

Towards the end of 1983, I was approached about the possibility of taking up a PR post in London and was eventually appointed. Roy and I talked about whether or not he would pull up his roots and move south with me. After initial enthusiasm, as the time drew nearer, he began to develop serious doubts about leaving Rotherham and his mother.

Some instinct told me that the problem was that he could not tell his mother or family why he should be moving to London with me (he had never mentioned being gay at home), and that that was mixed up with his profound sense of responsibility for supporting Vera.

I proposed that I should phone his sister and tell her exactly what the situation was so that Roy could then tackle the question with the issue out in the open. This he did, and was warmly supported by the family in his intention. He did, not, however, tell the whole truth to Vera, and she remained anxious about what she saw as Roy's fragile and dependent status: what would he do if I threw him out? she wondered.

For Roy, these discussions cleared the air, and he felt free to make the move. So, just six or seven months after we had met, we set off for London, and temporary residence on the floor of a friend's crowded dining-room in Barnes.

I started my new job, and, within days of our arrival, after briefly indulging the joys of unemployed freedom, Roy found a job as an assistant at Travellers' Fare at Paddington Station. After a few weeks he applied to London Transport and went back to bus driving. After handing in his notice at Travellers' Fare, they told him they had been about to promote him to supervisor.

I occasionally caught his bus on my way to work, and felt a huge, romantic thrill at seeing him at the wheel of a big red London bus, and at being one of his passengers: if only everyone else on the bus had known how lucky they were to have such a driver!

Between us we earned a pretty substantial sum, and we very rapidly established the self-indulgent habits that were to characterise our years together: eating and drinking out together and with friends, going to films and plays, clubbing it way into the small hours, and going abroad for holidays. We went to Harrods and bought nest-building things in the sale, walked by the Thames and took riverboat trips along it, sat in parks and had picnics, strolled happily along Oxford Street, and began to feel that the Great City was becoming home.

After six months of bedsit land, we found and bought a turn-of-the-century, three-bedroomed, terraced house in Balham and set about renovating and decorating it from top to bottom. Roy took a leading part in this substantial enterprise.

We had very similar nest-building instincts, and soon the house was transformed into a warmly comfortable, welcoming place, in which we felt at ease and in which our many guests had happy times with us. Each summer we had a great champagne party in the garden - an event which started at midday and usually went on into the following early morning - as well as many dinner parties and boozy evenings.

After a little while in the house, Roy decided he wanted to bring his beloved Lady down from Rotherham, and, though I was far from keen to have a dependent animal around, I raised no objection: he was devoted to her, and the house was, after all, as much his as mine.

I came to love the old black mongrel nearly as much as he, though I was, from time to time, feebly resentful of the affection and tenderness which he lavished on her, more of which I thought he might have directed towards me.

In a generally very harmonious life, we did have some mighty rows and struggles in the first couple of years as we went through the process of learning about each other and making all the adjustments and concessions which are necessary for two mature, independent people to live together.

I - for example - had a tendency to be very untidy and slovenly around the place, leaving newspapers and coffee cups, letters, clothes and any other movable items just where I had finished with them. It had been a huge personal liberation for me to be master of my own territory once I had left home and to behave just however I pleased. While in many ways I was an intensely organised and focused person, this studied neglect of order in the domestic world had become something of an obsession with me.

Roy had quite different ideas about how a house should be managed and expressed them strongly. Some childlike aspect of my personality reacted to this with angry resentment and we had several real rows when he tried to persuade me to put things away and keep the house in order. As time passed, I began to adopt his values and behaviour, and though there were real lapses from time to time, my standards were soon nearly as high as his. Those are habits which have never left me.

That same process of accommodation and growth took place for us both in all kinds of ways, many of them much subtler and more internal than the mere orderliness of the external world.

Our approaches to the spending of money were very different: he, from a well-managed, prudent, working class home saw money as something to be put aside for hard times; I from a financially comfortable background and several years of bachelorhood on a reasonable income spent practically everything I earned and saw that freedom as the reason for earning. Roy, however, took to the pleasure of spending money rather more quickly than I took to the habits of domestic tidiness: we did save, but, my goodness, we did spend too!

He had always had a great appetite for pleasure. The dramatic move from Rotherham - with all the opportunities and new experiences it opened up - reinforced and developed that to an adventurousness which was quite astonishing, and which occasionally made me feel cautious and conservative. He would try out new foods, new music, new cultural experiences, new friends and would almost always emerge satisfied and hankering for more.

Socially he was enormously competent and people of every age and background and type responded with warmth and affection to him - he had the most catholic circle of friends of anyone I knew or know now. He had no time at all for the superficial or pretentious, and quickly assessed who was to be taken seriously and who to be avoided for good. In many ways he was socially more adaptable and generous than I, and though we both maintained a few friends more or less independently, our mutual circle flourished, most often through new contacts he had made.

He was not in any sense an intellectual, though he had great natural intelligence, judgment and perception. My more serious, academic side was not something which was explicitly part of our mutual life. He was proud, I think, that I was a published writer, and encouraged me to continue writing, but he never read any of my books or articles - nor indeed anyone else's, I think.

My social work background had left me with a legacy of beliefs about how healthy human relationships should be conducted, some of which had proved valuable and durable. One of these was the principle of 'talking through' conflicts and difficulties as a way of restoring harmony. It's a very sound principle, and highly effective in many circumstances, but I learnt from Roy that there are other ways of dealing with conflict that are often equally, if not more effective.

If there were anger or resentment in the air, my inclination was (sometimes after hours or days of brooding) to broach the subject and start a mutual inquisition as to what was happening. There were times when this was the best way for both of us (it was usually me who took the bull by the horns) - but there were many occasions when it wasn't the way at all. Roy taught me that anger (for example) can be expressed as the feeling of the moment and then be utterly forgotten. If my response to such an expression was to brood and sulk for ages, then I was making something out of the event which was entirely unbalanced in relation to his feeling or wishes. That robustness, that availability of spontaneity and of forward movement, was typical of him and from it I learnt a great deal.

He found tenderness much more difficult to express in words and there were times when I, with my particular attachment to verbal communication, found that quite difficult to endure. He knew it, and occasionally acknowledged it, and I came to accept that, in general it was not his way. His granite loyalty and commitment were so evident in action, why did I need the words as well?

It was only in the first year or two, and then only briefly, that we had any problems about sexual matters, and they stemmed from my enthusiasm for a number of bars and a raunchy night sauna in Amsterdam. It was a place I had visited several times before Roy and I met, and it had provided me with some of the most delicious and memorable sexual experiences of my life, at a time when I had been just discovering how exciting sex with another man could be.

Roy had previously been on a brief holiday to Amsterdam with a mixed group of friends, but had discovered nothing of the astonishing gay life of the City. On our first visit together (the first of many) I wanted him to go to the sauna with me, but he decided it was not for him and was clearly not at all keen for me to go on my own. I went and next day, rather insensitively, told him all about the night's events. It was my way, I think, of indicating that I did not feel that whatever might have happened was significant or to be seen as intruding on our relationship. In retrospect I think I was imprudent and probably hurtful.

During later visits to the City, however, things were very different. We would go to the sauna together, sit for a while drinking at the bar or sweating in one of the cabins, and then go off separately, to meet an hour or so later and swop stories over a beer. The routine might be repeated three or four times before we would walk home together in the light of the dawn, feeling content and at peace. With the exception of these early indulgences (which took place only in Amsterdam), and two later, separate occasions of infidelity, we were both faithful.

Music was one area to which we both opened doors for each other. I was a dilletante dabbler in modern and pop music, but didn't know much about it, and hadn't really collected records or tapes much since the days of the

Beatles. I enjoyed pop music, particularly for dancing, but was quite out of touch with the modern scene. Roy had a tremendous collection of records and tapes which he renewed with purchases every time he heard something he liked. Listening to music was as integral a part of his life as reading the Guardian every day was of mine. He could happily spend hours with his headphones on and a drink in his hand.

He taught me to take popular music seriously and to find real pleasure in musicals and light musical entertainment - to understand that it was often not just frothy, lightweight, trivial entertainment, but a serious expression of real and profound feeling. 'I am what I am' was probably his absolute favourite song, and it represented the expression of his deepest feelings about life - live with pride, confidence, extravagance and colour whatever the odds or the objections: how could one not be profoundly moved by such a commitment?

And for him, I opened the door on classical music, which he came to love and listen to of his own accord. Seeking a gentle first experience of opera for us both, we saw the Magic Flute at the Coliseum and were both completely entranced by the production. We saw it twice more, bought the CD, and played it endlessly at home. He loved it.

He danced and sang in two or three musicals produced by the London Transport Players, and flourished in grease-paint and costume, though in the end withdrew because of the bitchy relationships and authoritarian style of some of the organisers. But costume he loved.

Knowing that he had a liking for drag, I had, very early in our relationship, bought him a pair of size eleven patent leather stilettos with six-inch heels. These remained a prized possession, to be brought out and tried at parties by even the butchest of our straight male friends, and worn by Roy whenever there was a suitable opportunity for exhibitionism. (One of the heels eventually snapped off under the weight of some hefty male, and it never got repaired.) At one of our summer parties, he emerged into the garden in a slinky black number belonging to one of our petite, slim girlfriends, a broad-brimmed hat, cigarette holder and fishnet stockings - and of course the stilettos. (Our slim friend was never able to wear the frock again.)

This was an aspect of him I was never quite at ease with, and I'm unsure why - whether it was because I was envious of his making such progress to liberation or afraid of finding I liked it too much, I don't know. His general appearance and behaviour were anything but camp, yet he could camp it up wonderfully when the mood took him. There were one or two of our girlfriends who were only too happy to indulge him with make-up, clothes and an appreciative audience, and I suspect his best drag nights were with them in my absence. I did not mind, indeed was pleased that what I had difficulty in offering he could find elsewhere.

We frequently went out for nights on the town, ending up at bars or clubs with drag shows, and there were a couple of acts we followed enthusiastically round the circuit: they were outrageous nights of happy, drunken, abandoned hilarity which I am sure I would never have considered let alone discovered without Roy.

I had always been a keen and committed cook, preparing lengthy and elaborate meals for my friends, something which Roy found perplexing in the early days: eating for him had been largely a swift, utilitarian activity. Over the years we became an incredibly accomplished team at providing hospitality, often spending a whole day preparing every last detail of a feast for ten or a dozen friends, and then, after they had gone, washing and clearing up everything before we went to bed. Even for ourselves, on a birthday or at Christmas, we would provide a feast, with the table fully decorated, flowers, candles, silver and linen, lingering for hours over the meal. I have the happiest memories of some of those intimate, indulgent domestic occasions.

After driving for a year or so, Roy applied for and was appointed as an Assistant Security Supervisor at London Transport's headquarters in Victoria. His principal duties were to work at the reception desk, signing staff and visitors in, answering enquiries, receiving parcels, and so on. He was a tremendous success at this, his warm, welcoming smile and courteous manner very rapidly making him popular with most of the hundreds of staff in the building. His attitude to Chairman or cleaner was just the same - mature, chatty, humorous, though there were some of the directors and managers whose attitude to him (and to humanity in general) used to make him furious.

For a short while, before Roy went to the headquarters building, I had had a senior PR post there, but it had come to a painful and wretched end with dire conflict with my boss, whom I, and many of her staff regarded as unpredictable and tyrannical. I secured two months' salary in lieu of notice, but Roy and I had to face the possibility of very dramatic changes in our lives. Through this major crisis (and others that were to follow) Roy provided incredible strength and comfort.

For him, the crisis was a crucial turning point in his self-confidence and self-image within our relationship. Previously, I had been the major earner (we could both have survived on my salary) and, virtually unconsciously, I think, he had been left feeling less than an equal partner. However much I might have protested that what was mine was his, and that we were an equal partnership, for him, especially from his background, status and responsibility within a household were deeply connected with earning capacity and actual responsibility exercised. He had, without question, taken an equal or more than equal part in almost all the practical aspects of maintaining our home and in nurturing our partnership, but it was he who followed me to London for my new job and it was he who had been unemployed (even if only for a matter of days) while I brought home the wage-packet.

Now, it was he who was bringing in the income to keep us in our home and to feed us; it was I who was out of work. There was no sense of relish in this, and, at the time, I am not sure we quite realised how important a process of change was taking place, but it strengthened him and banished whatever lingering sense of inequality he felt.

I managed to build up a successful freelance PR consultancy, working from home, and was then recruited as a director of a small advertising agency in south

London. During that time we moved to a larger, four-bedroomed, 1890s terraced house half a mile from where we had first lived. There was a bigger garden and, beyond it, the open spaces of the Common.

After three years or so, that company went into liquidation and, once again, it was Roy who provided the steady strength and income through crisis. There was the real risk that we would lose the house if the liquidation evolved badly, and we had to face the stark realities of possible homelessness. This we did by facing the worst possible case which, we imagined, was setting up a tent on Clapham Common and waiting for something to turn up. As so often happens, staring the worst in the face makes one realise that it's not the end of the world, and that one might as well carry on without despair. He was just great, miserable and angry though he was some of the time about the causes of the disaster. We had lost thirty-five thousand pounds in the collapse, and it was I who had promoted the investment. There were no recriminations.

We went abroad once or twice a year: several times to Amsterdam, to California, Jersey, Barcelona and Seville, Rome; weekend and day trips to Scandinavia or France and had two magical holidays in remotest north west Scotland.

There we rented keepers' lodges, dozens of miles from evidence of civilisation, with little but sheep, deer, soaring birds of prey and the wild, unpredictable weather to absorb our attention. The cottages had electricity (the remoter one had a generator), open fires, and were set in wild, unfenced valleys covered with heather and rocky outcrops, one near the sea, the other on the bank of a loch. We were bewitched by the magic of the place, the silence, the peacefulness of it, and the wonderfully uplifting, natural rhythms one's mind and body quickly adopt without the demands of routines, telephones and mundane, everyday activities.

Our second holiday we shared with a girlfriend Nicky, Roy's most valued and intimate companion outside our relationship. We cooked huge breakfasts and dinners, baked bread and scones, sat around reading by the light of the fire, talked, dozed, walked, visited remote, blustery beaches, ate venison, haggis and fresh salmon, drank wine and whisky, stayed up half the night, and slept long into the mornings. It was an immensely enriching and happy time.

Roy remained loyal and committed to Vera and visited her two or three times a year. Sometimes we would go together for a Bank Holiday, on other occasions he travelled alone and stayed for a few days. In the early years we went to Rotherham for Christmas, though I rather resented this as I had long established the habit of spending Christmas with chosen friends in the place I regarded as my home. I fulfilled my duties, I hope, with good grace, and was, in any case, touched by the warmth and generosity of my reception: Vera was always the most liberal and amusing of hostesses.

One year the compromise was for Roy's family all to come to stay with us for Christmas, and we compounded the achievement by having my family along on Boxing Day as well. It all went off very successfully and the change in the annual routine paved the way for us eventually to have

Christmas on our own, as we both truly wanted. Between Christmas and New Year we then visited both our families for a couple of days.

From our first visit to my parents in Northamptonshire, I was very touched by the warmth of their welcome for Roy, and they, and my brother, sister-in-law and young nephews, became very fond of him. My parents' positive reaction to the incontrovertible fact of our partnership did much to strengthen my already healing bonds with them.

With my brother, sister-in-law and the two boys, we had a wonderful week's holiday on a narrow boat on the canals of the East Midlands, pottering along at four miles an hour and stopping at regular intervals for gin and tonic and lengthy and sumptuous meals.

That holiday, and many of the others, provided Roy with rich opportunity for observing and enjoying animals and natural things. We never passed a beach with a rockpool or a patch of water without Roy being on his haunches peering into the depths, lifting stones and rocks, endlessly absorbed and fascinated by anything that moved or grew.

At home we had Lady, of course, but there was also lots of other livestock. The zoology was his preserve, and though I helped out, particularly with feeding and walking the dog, I did make it clear that while I enjoyed the collection, I was not willing to carry much of the responsibility for it.

What could it be that made two such very different men find such extraordinary and lasting pleasure in each other? I'm not sure that I am very much clearer even after writing this, nor, to take from Roy's wisdom, that it greatly matters whether it can be put into words or not. The answers may be more apparent to a reader than they are to me.

What I do know is that there was wonderful compatibility in our general disposition towards life: our inclination was always to say yes if something promising was offered; our habit was never to do things by halves. We loved food and drink and the society of friends; travel delighted us both and we were, simply, happy in each other's company. There was also compatibility in our differences: we were able to learn from each other and change the ways we had felt or reacted in the past to new ways; and such things as we couldn't or didn't wish to share we were happy to accept and leave alone, and provide space for the other to pursue and enjoy.

The great and overwhelming memory I have is what I think was mutual, unconditional love: it was rarely expressed, but it was the groundrock on which our happiness was built. After perhaps a year or so of being together it became increasingly potent: we were together for life; there was to be no-one else, no rivals, no alternatives, this was it, willingly and completely. It was in the warm liberation of that commitment that I think we were both able to flourish. It was in that same strength that, together, we were able to adapt to the trials of chronic illness and to the knowledge of certain death.

And still, it warms and sustains and liberates my new life without him.

The DIARY

Part I: February 1990-June 1991

Part II: Round the World July-August 1991

Part III: September 1991-February 1992

Part IV: March 1992

Part V: April-September 1992

These five sections contain almost the complete text of the contemporary diary which I kept and to which Roy made some contributions. It appears almost entirely unedited, just as it was written at all hours of the day and night in whatever mental and physical state prevailed at the time. There is also some additional explanatory material which was written more recently, which appears in italics.

The Round the World section was composed as a narrative two years after the event from comprehensive notes dictated during the trip.

Roy, early sixties: caravan holidays and the family's motorbike and sidecar

Sun, sea and sand - with an early shot at driving

The DIARY

PART I

February 1990 - June 1991

Roy loved living things. He had a great appetite for the company of human beings, and a fascination with every kind of animal, bird and fish, and plants, flowers and trees too. During our time together he had canaries and zebra finches; tropical and pond fish; rabbits and guinea pigs; and, of course, the love of his life, Lady.

Lady was a gentle, dependent, lovable black mongrel Roy's grandfather had found abandoned as a puppy - wrapped in newspaper on his Yorkshire doorstep in the mid-seventies. After his grandfather's death, Roy in his teens adopted her and was always besotted. She moved to London with us in 1984 and had been with us for nearly seven years. She was about 15 at this time, and becoming progressively weak and ill.

I had had great reservations about her living with us: I did not relish the commitment, the restriction of freedom, the walking, the feeding, the demands and responsibilities.

Perhaps I didn't want the competition for his attention either. But she was so essential to his happiness, that I

Top String for balloons - our first meeting autumn 1983
Left Booze cruise on the North Sea, winter 1983
Centre A handsome bus driver, before we met
Right Our first morning after, 1983

Holiday shots 1985-88

could not stand in the way of her arrival. I was occasionally irritated by her insatiable craving for attention and Roy's evident capacity to express to her the tenderness he found difficult to show me, but I soon became very fond of her and valued the profound contribution she made to Roy's happiness.

It had been evident for months that she was declining physically. Cleaning up trails of mess when we returned home in the evenings became commonplace, but it still took us a long time and lots of ultimately fruitless visits to the vet to come to the inevitable decision.

17 February: Today we said goodbye to Lady. It was ever so sad and we cried a lot. We still expect to see her around, and look behind us for that ever-present shadow wherever we go. It's strange and silent without her. Roy, wretched but resolved, stayed in bed on the morning of the day of execution and could not bear to come, so I walked her across the common to the surgery, tears in my eyes all the way. While my resolve did not waver, I felt treacherous. She resisted every step of the journey. The vet was kind, perceptive, helpful, and the end was swift and gentle. They had tissues on hand for bereaved owners to mop their tears.

It was very hard for me; I cannot begin to imagine how hard for Roy. Although her body was wasting, those wide eyes never changed - that look of doleful expectation and anticipation; that unqualified, ineffable affection and trust.

But it was time. The vet said her heart would keep her going even into complete physical incapacity. And she was long past the stage of ever being physically relaxed. She was bumping into things and having more and more trouble getting onto chairs or up the stairs. She never really settled anywhere except occasionally dozing with Roy on the sofa. She wandered about aimlessly, sometimes simply staring blankly at the wall; her muscles and her body wasting. And the mess!

Roy said today that, if anything, we'd left the decision late - but what could we do when there was even a remote chance of improvement? Delay was better than rushing in. We had lots of good times with her. She had a happy and full life. She had enriched Roy's life beyond measure.

In retrospect, Lady's death takes on a significance it did not have at the time: it was not only the absolute end of an era in our lives - the era of carefree confidence and careless expectation of growing old together - but also a marker of the passing of more than 90% of Roy's lifespan. Only three weeks later we had the cataclysmic news of another imminent death in the family.

At this time, Roy was a member of the security team - working mostly at the reception desk - at London Transport's HQ in Victoria, a post in which he was capable and tolerably content. While he was often infuriated by corporate silliness and individual pretension or discourtesy, there was lots of opportunity for making friends and for gossip and quiet entertainment. He made many friends among the hundreds of staff and visitors.

For some months he'd not been really well, particularly troubled by a persistent cough and occasional painful sinusitis. He was never bad enough to have time off work,

Forces of law and order: Roy and Ian, 1988

Canal boat holiday 1988
Top Roy and Lady
Bottom With Bruce's brother Iain and Andrew and Mark

but it had been going on long enough for him to visit his GP, who'd taken blood samples to check out the infection.

I had been increasingly unhappy in my employment at a West End advertising agency where I had been recruited after the disastrous liquidation of my previous employer and a period of freelance consultancy. Thinking of starting up my own company, I had the immense good fortune of a long-term client of mine offering to put up substantial capital for the enterprise. Gathering a number of capable professional friends around me, all of whom also put up money for the business, we were in the very early stages of putting together the business plan which would lead to the birth of our own consultancy in the summer of this year. It was a tremendous opportunity and challenge - taken up when, as it turned out, hanging on to a secure salary might have been the more rational and prudent choice.

Much of my then current and future work took me off on trips round the UK, delivering training sessions, planning marketing and PR campaigns and lots more. The enormous demands of setting up a new business and of constant periods away from home were to prove very hard to manage in the months ahead.

* * * *

8 March: I was in Cirencester for the day. On the way home, I met a colleague at Kings Cross to discuss some business and have a few drinks. I got home mid-evening, rather pissed, after calling on the mobile to let Roy know what was happening. He gave no inkling of the news to come.

He was sat bolt upright in bed and asked me to sit down. He'd been called to the clinic and given all the blood test results. He was HIV+.

We had talked before about this possible result, but had kept up our hopes with 'glandular fever' which had been the GP's best shot.

It is almost impossible to take in the meaning: for Roy, being told was like being suddenly given a disease - though nothing had physically changed; knowledge precipitated us into a new understanding of the present; revolutionised everything. This had been the reality all along, but we had not known it.

We have reacted and talked as if he is about to die. We are busily sorting out wills, insurance policies and so on; already I have experienced this lovely home of ours as if he were not here - the ordinary everyday things which he sees, uses, which are part of our life together. I have felt his loss and cried. I have held him in my arms, slept with him, and felt the desperation, the insupportable sense of his not being there; the ending of that dear, warm, loving dependable being with whom I have built my anchor, my home, my security.

At first we agreed to tell no one. That irrational and fearful shock-reaction has subsided and, thinking of our friends, we soon felt there were few, if any, who did not have the knowledge, balance and kindness which would make telling them a relief and a comfort. Secrecy would only intensify our sadness; sharing will relieve and comfort, help us to come to terms.

We are not ashamed or guilty: we've been largely careful and prudent - we have not been careless or irresponsible, but

The later years together
Top At the gate of our second home in Balham (1991)
Middle Visiting a castle in Framlingham with the Hawksleys (1990)
Bottom A Northamptomshire lane with nephew Andrew and brother Iain's
Morgan (1990)

Top Vera with Roy at home in Balham
Left Roy and Nicky above Loch More (1989)
Right An extravagant afternoon party in our first home in Balham: Roy shows
off the stils, supported by the Divine Miss Lodge (1985)

our defences were not complete - whose can be? Who knows what encounter opened the door and when? It is of no consequence - it is all too long ago.

The question of my being tested arises - a curious kind of comfort and companionship, a reduction of anxiety should I be positive too - and there has to be at least an even chance. But if I am not, a realistic approach to sensible prevention. I am not keen on anything that separates us. But don't we have enough to worry us?

In recent months I think we have been getting closer and closer - Lady's going was a time of extraordinary intimacy and mutual support - I think we grew a lot through that. We've had our crises, but my goodness, we've had our good times too! Our friend Mark said last night, 'You've lived at the cutting edge of life!' - and while I felt that that perhaps over-stated or romanticised it a bit, we've done very well.

We've spoken much about our past together, now in the (still not fully-realised) certainty of its ending. We've not wasted our time together - through all the dark nights of losing jobs, business collapsing, we've not just stuck together, but become more and more intimately woven together. Roy has been a tower of strength in every way - emotional, practical, reliably earning his wage (anyone who doesn't see his great, essential strength doesn't understand this partnership!)

And we've built two wonderful homes together - here, especially, such a lovely, reassuring, kindly place which in its twenty months or so has already welcomed and pleased so many dozens of friends, family, visitors. It makes a possible ending so much more deeply sad, and at the same time, less terrible, though terrible it is.

I cannot begin to imagine what it must be like now for Roy to live with this knowledge - so little shows on the outside. He has talked of the sensation of the alien organism in his body, of the tunnel at the end of which the light, if it is light, is an ending - though both of us know that he may have years of healthy life.

The possibility of HIV had clearly crossed his mind during his awful flu/cold/sinusitis/cough - which went on so long, so painfully. The first local blood test results were badly handled by the receptionist: low platelets. Retest. What on earth did that mean? And though the second set appeared at first to be OK, the doctor's telephone consultation with a colleague produced the response, 'Nothing to worry about if he's heterosexual.' (What ignorance and prejudice did that reveal, for god's sake? Did this chap imagine disease was influenced by the sexual-orientation of its host?)

So began the path to James Pringle House and the Middlesex Hospital and this staggering change in our consciousness. It can never go away. We live with it for always.

And yet we know also, once this period of shock (and perhaps still unclimaxed crisis) is over, we must, above all, continue as normal, live positively, plan for the future, arrange holidays - and, with continuing spontaneity and a little contrivance, do all those things that we want to do sooner rather than later.

At the moment I feel uneasy out of his presence - I went shopping today and was anxious not being with him. Tonight, he's out with friends, I worried, just worried because I wasn't with him. Next week I am in Derby and am anxious about being away. I have to remind myself he's not going to disappear in a puff of smoke. Everything feels so fragile.

I feel proud that we're part of the caring, helpful, practical network of the gay community - we can't look to more conventional networks for the support we need. (Our own friends - yes; family difficult, especially parents; the great world outside - apparently hostile and detached. One comfort - the clinic has already been splendid.)

We have so much ground to cover together - in terms of adjusting to this new reality and in the things we must do together.

We are certain we want to keep the home going - attractive though the prospect of selling up and sailing round the world might be, we need the anchor, the resource, the pleasure of home. If either of us is going to be ill - let it be here.

And then we come on to the other startling development of 1990 which makes one wonder about the convergence of events, the remarkable balance of positive and (apparently) negative, the extraordinary cycle of life's pattern: the gestation of a new a ambitious creature to be born in the not too-distant future: EQUUS, as we've decided my new company is to be called.

The keeping of our diary was, as so often with good intentions, sporadic. Off and on over the years, we had kept diaries of periods of weeks or months, but they did little except record events. We were living life at such a pace that there was little time for reflection and in-depth record-keeping. However, from the time of the diagnosis until well after his death, I sat down quite frequently and committed the thoughts and feelings of the day to paper. Roy, occasionally, and reluctantly contributed, though the written word had never been his medium.

His entries - usually brief - throw some light on his reactions and feelings. They are often allusive and understated, even seeming naive, but they are the markers of a deeply reflective, intelligent, responsive mind and personality which rarely disclosed their complexity in mere words.

Analysis was not his medium either, while words were and are the principal means through which I experience life and make sense of it (though less dominantly so since I met him). While he taught me that words were very often far less significant that actions and evidence, he did not learn from me the exploratory, intellectually playful, subversive or neurotic uses of words which were so much my stock in trade. He had the deepest and most passionate of feelings, but one could best feel them through empathy rather than listening. Our arguments in the early days were complicated by the fact that he was expressing plain feelings and I was expressing the unreliable verbalisation of feelings that were far from plain.

He had a considerable wit and sense of humour which he expressed through real verbal dexterity, often laced with the catch-phrases and colloquialisms of broad Yorkshire. (One of his favourites: of anything that was rapidly rising and falling - like his temperature from time to time - he'd say: 'Up and *down like a whoor's drawers.') He was very funny indeed, often at the expense of human foibles.*

He valued and appreciated aspects of my verbal and written facility when I was able to express feelings which he might otherwise have let lie. He was a connoisseur of my frequent letters of complaint on his behalf and my own. These were usually written after some outrage had been perpetrated upon us by some abusive or ignorant service person or shop or restaurant. I would draft letters and documents for him to a standard he could never have matched, but he was able to apply his considerable intelligence to modify and refine them.

At some of the most difficult times - most notably telling his family about our intention to leave Yorkshire and to live in London; and, much later that he was gay and seriously ill - he wanted me to speak for him and for us both.

Here is the first of his few entries during this time. It poignantly illustrates, among much else, the frustration he sometimes felt at his inability to express tenderness to me.

* * * *

12 March Roy's entry: Well, what can I say - I am feeling very much like Bruce has been doing - we've had our ups and a fair share of downs, but in spite of everything we've stuck together closely, I think, in times of crisis.

Though I don't do it consciously, I can't stop thinking what the future holds or doesn't - I hate being away from Bruce even for a few minutes - time that previously we, well me certainly, took for granted and on occasions abused - I used to get annoyed and after a while look in Bruce's direction and see his hurt profile and inside I would shed a tear and my annoyance would go seeming so trivial and ridiculous and unimportant.

It is difficult really to decide how I feel except vulnerable and strangely small - no longer feeling in control of events - I feel as though I've got to fall into events and take them as they come along - there's not been a complete night's rest it seems like for weeks - better for being with Bruce giving me comfort and relief but woke up last night thinking this cannot be - why me? - can't be true, etc. The only logical way of sorting that out is if you're playing with fire expect to get singed - but that doesn't help, certainly doesn't make me feel better.

Can't help thinking what the end will be or what hoops I'm going to be put through in the meantime - I've never been afraid of death, only the circumstance surrounding it, but now all of a sudden it has been presented to me and I'm frightened, totally frightened. What should I do? Carry on smoking though it's not helping, carry on drinking? If I don't it may give a little longer - to what end? These are the thoughts I'm trying to avoid but back they always come, thundering back.

I'm trying my best not to indulge in self-pity, but come to the conclusion if I can't do it now, when can I?

Though he could have been on sick leave for most of his last two years, he stayed at work until only months before he died. Unless he was actually incapacitated or in hospital he continued to get up and go out, day after day.

Occasionally, we managed to take time together either on holiday, or, as recorded in the next entries, on short business trips when he accompanied me or joined me. These had a particular sweetness as they were little triumphs over the business imperative which usually separated us. They were also quite ordinary experiences shared and relished in the light of our new knowledge of shortening perspectives.

This early period saw our minds constantly processing the new realities and coming to the increasingly vivid realisation that what we had to do was live for the present and the very short-term. This was only one stage beyond what had always been our instincts, but it was still a giant threshhold to cross.

* * * *

15 March Roy's entry: Not long since got back from extremely enjoyable evening yesterday and today with Bruce in Derby while he was visiting customers. Had excellent evening meal in hotel and long time chatting and drinking. Slept quite well - the booze probably had something to do with it!

Quite an early start today. Set off for Buxton via excellent countryside with greenery and flowers bursting out all over. In Buxton Bruce went to work while I went to walk through the glasshouses and gardens - loads of ducks and people pottering around - very relaxed! Of course ended up in the pottery and craft centre. Went into a very nice lavender blue shop and bought - yet another! - vase. Will eventually need a removal van to take all the vases down to the Antiques Roadshow! Met Bruce again at 12:30 and off we set back - only took it steady but lots of hold-ups owing to roadworks. Popped into a cafe en route back - Bruce had two eggs and chips and I had fish and chips and peas with doorstop bread and butter. All sorts of chattels everywhere - big dog, parrot, Happy Shopper clock and a set of fairy lights above the door that I think Adam put up - so ancient!

Got back to Derby early afternoon and caught train at 15:00 - Bruce going off back to work unfortunately. The time together has been wonderful and I didn't want the day to end. Felt quite upset on parting.

Thought for today - still trying not to think about it but still finding it difficult not to choke up occasionally.

15 March: Our week together has been very comforting and affectionate - even with my being away. It was wonderful that he came up to Derby - long, peaceful evening together, a short lie-in together in the morning, shower, breakfast and a drive in a lovely bright morning to Buxton. I did not wish to return to work!

We talked frequently on the phone. He walked down to meet me from the tube - a lovely surprise and we've had another peaceful, communicative evening. I've left our bed with an overactive brain in the middle of the night, and have typed up a statement for us to sign at the solicitors next week and am now catching up on the diary.

The need to record things (more even than usual!) is part, I think, of our renewed determination to relish each day, to value and remember - though Roy has suggested it might make a best-seller (he's as bad as me!)

We've been able to laugh too - Roy imagining the domestic chaos I'll inhabit when his guiding hand is no longer around - will he return, rattling his chains like Marley, to empty the dishwasher and mop the kitchen floor?

Tonight he talked of feeling 'cheated' - because he feels the crucial (infectious) event took place before he knew there was danger, before the many years when he was so careful. The feeling's real enough, but it gets us nowhere.

He suggested we should go away for more weekends - get about, see places he's never seen. We must certainly not waste our time together. But our daily intimacy is the greatest comfort - I hope it is for him. We are being tested, and the foundations we've laid over the years are proving deep and firm.

He seemed surprised that I am still aroused by him - that his health status is not offputting - but it is so clear that there is no change in him to me (and yet there is such change). Such things are not for him now, how could they be?

I spoke to Jenny my sister-in-law tonight, and she was kind and level-headed and asked us to stay with them. We spoke of her arthritis and that prompted Roy and me to think about the prospect of a lifelong, painful, crippling disease - the wheelchair, the daily pain. Die young and quick rather than that! Was it worse for those left after the death of an aged loved one or a younger loved one? Perhaps the emptiness after the loss of lifelong habits and companionship was worse? The best - of course - to go quickly and easily together - a kind of orgasm, Roy bizarrely remarked!

It's a great relief that our conversation seems largely relaxed and uninhibited - we are not afraid of the issues, and the emotions are well under control.

I think I've dealt with the tragic aspects by keeping them largely out of mind - though the fact's ever with me and, from time to time, I'm overcome with misery at the remotest glimpse of the empty house, or the bed without his warm, palpable breathing presence. I cannot afford to let myself imagine it.

There is so much to do in the next few weeks - apart from what we must do together - if the business is to get going, if there is to be a positive break with my previous employer - yet holding onto some cash, some work, some security?

Since Roy pointed out the irony of 'positive' I cannot use it without reluctance: 'Be positive!' they say in facing life: can any word have had such a profound irony?

I must to bed. I want to make good use of the weekend. Next week we meet with the solicitors, our executors (my brother and Roy's brother-in-law), to tie up our affairs and make formal and as near to legal as possible our determination that no one beyond the two of us can interfere in the integrity of our mutual finances, responsibilities and commitment, whatever may happen. The fear may be an over-reaction, but the world can be hostile and uncaring enough for us to have good reason to be cautious.

Our reactions to the news in this first week were relatively moderate, uncannily so in some respects. However, we were about to experience an emotional eruption which was altogether more proportionate to the drama. Unusually, it was Roy who was to be the subject of this assault of anger and despair and I who was to be vicariously purged.

The Saturday of this week, Roy was going out for the evening with Ian and Katie, a young couple he'd met through work with whom we'd had lots of extravagant, boozy, happy times at their flat in Hammersmith, in town, at mutual friends' and at our place. They were relaxed and affectionate people who had many gay friends and were very easy with human idiosyncrasy. Some drama was to surface much later as their relationship crumbled, but there were no outward signs of trouble at this stage. They'd been together for several years since university.

Roy and I maintained some degree of social independence and on this occasion he was going out with them on his own. We had not yet told them the news.

* * * *

16 March: I must return to last Saturday the point at which the revellers returned. Roy was obviously very pissed - being led up the path by pale and anxious looking Katie. I greeted Ian over-effusively, not seeing the pain and anxiety in his face - not knowing they knew. Roy collapsed on the stairs, pale and soon weeping. Ian and Katie went into the front room, and I closed the door through which sounds of extravagant grief soon came. Roy was desolate, apologetic, eventually - in the kitchen - bitterly angry, raging about 'bastard life' that had sought him out for such a fate.

During the next few hours the four of us sat together in each other's arms, formed changing couples in the sitting room and the kitchen all (except me this night) frequently in floods of gasping tears.

It was the deepest extravagance of grief I've ever been close to, and at the same time the most passionate, beautiful declaration of love for Roy - Ian said it over and over again - how much Roy (and I) meant to them both, how his life had been changed by meeting Roy since he came to London, how much they both loved him.

In the taxi home they had both - over Roy's more or less unconscious form - wondered with desperation which of their dear friends would be next - a catalogue of terrifying possibilities.

Everyone kept apologising - Ian for his tears, Roy for being 'the cause' - in a way which was sadly British - because everyone was actually dealing with their shock, anger and grief just about as heroically and beautifully as they could - and with passionate spontaneity.

Katie and Ian were booked on a 9am flight to Paris - they didn't leave here till 3am or later.

It was a night of despairing grief for Roy: he said he felt he did not have long left, and was so vulnerable, helpless, hopeless. We eventually went to bed together and slept.

It was the night of the deepest realisation and expression of the crisis - a wild collision with the truth as it was inside for Roy and outside in the world - passionately represented by Ian and Katie.

Roy stayed late in bed on Sunday, waking much calmer - with only a patchy memory of the night - and said he felt better. I lingered with him, finding it hard to focus my mind on anything else - but had to prepare myself for the business meeting with my colleagues that afternoon, had to collect myself, control the ache in my throat, and the tears which constantly threatened to stop me in my tracks.

The next week we had a meeting with our solicitors in Sheffield. My brother Iain and Roy's brother-in-law Bill were there as executors of both our wills.

We had updated our wills (they had been written originally under the influence of the naive assumption that I would obviously die first, though there were provisions in the event of a reversal of usual expectations); we signed them and had them witnessed; we signed and had witnessed mutual Enduring Powers of Attorney; we read out and signed a declaration for attachment to our wills.

This called upon anyone who might be concerned in our affairs to treat Roy and me as nearest of next of kin in all respects - financial, inheritance, access to each other or information about each other, and so on - as if we were related by primary blood-ties or were married. We also included a section from the Euthanasia Society's Living Will which requests that, in terminal illness, life should not be fruitlessly prolonged and that pain should be effectively managed even if death is hastened.

Given our unconditional commitment to each other, we had been alarmed at the possibility of others not accepting or respecting our wishes, given that there was no watertight method for formal, legal recognition of our relationship.

We had heard stories of gay partners being refused rights of access to visit in hospital or to medical information; of families removing the body and not involving the partner in the funeral; of houses and belongings being repossessed. We did not suspect our families were capable of such brutality, but the world was sufficiently unpredictable for us to take every possible precaution.

As it happened, no one at any time ever challenged our rights and wishes, but we had done everything reasonably possible and were relieved and comfortable in the knowledge.

Around this time, Roy went off to Rotherham to visit Vera. He left the house while I was out. I returned to find a pink rose and a sweet note on my desk. It prompted me to write a piece describing the effects of the diagnosis on our lives.

When Roy saw it he was pleased and thought it might help others going through similar experiences. I sent it off to Gay Times and it was published later in the summer. (The text appears on page 253)

* * * *

17 March Roy's entry: Just sat down after a day in the garden - cleaned out the rabbit and birds, planted several bowls of bulbs which appear to have given up in the house, repotted yukka - hopefully that'll now stand up. Bruce just phoned - he caught same train as me yesterday, so he'll be home anytime.

Thought for today: feeling a lot more (what an ironical term) positive - felt awake and quite with-it - not been dwelling on the subject.

Holidays had always been a particular pleasure for us. Roy always found endless things to amuse him - not least the rockpools and wildlife of seaside and mountain - and we were both capable of that lazy serendipity which makes exploring new places so rich. We'd been to remote

spots in Scotland, on narrow-boats with my brother and his
family, to Amsterdam several times, to Jersey, Rome,
Barcelona and Seville (southern Spain was just too hot for
Roy), and dreamed comfortably of more exotic locations.
This time it was to be five days in Amsterdam.

The great city was cool and misty much of the time, but
no less bewitching for that, though the temperature was less
than comfortable for Roy in a slightly fragile state, and we
had some rough patches between us.

* * * *

18 April: We returned here at about 9:30pm last evening
after our five nights and five days in Amsterdam. As always
it's been a memorable, rich and full holiday in an excellent
city where we feel very much at home. Certainly, this
morning in London, I feel that I have now arrived in a very
foreign country!

Not only have we done and seen a great deal but it's been
a holiday with time of great intensity - both of pleasure and
on a couple of occasions some tension and conflict - which,
happily we recovered from quickly. It was much to do with
conflicting moods and priorities, our inner lives and needs
being less harmonious and predictable just now. We had to
walk round each other very delicately for a time.

Except for one day, Roy was not on form, prone to
tiredness, especially as the evening progresses, and has had
some stomach discomfort - though we've eaten and drunk
hugely.

Without rushing at all, we've done a great deal and seen
many sights we've not visited before (particularly Botanical

Gardens and nearby markets; fascinated to see entire bridge-section of major road over a canal (including pavement and street-lights) rise to let ships through).

18 April Roy's entry: Generally good holiday, but couldn't really cope with going out in evenings. I'd had enough through the day, smoky bars and generally not actually wanting to drink made evenings hard work. Day of departure felt lousy - glad to be back at home and in bed.

5 May: It's Saturday, the first day of the bank holiday - and it's beautiful - warm, bright, summery - a gently small breeze - birds singing, everything vigorous and in full growth - and peaceful - inner and outer - it seems for the first time for ages.

Life has been an absolute whirl for weeks - visits to customers round the country, the demands of the office, hectic getting the new business underway - there's so much to do, though the team is really starting to take the weight.

Roy has been in good form - though quickly tired, unpredictable sleep, some sweats, and tummy trouble, drinking less alcohol, eating OK - bearing up. It's difficult to know what to make of it, and I don't know if all this frenzy with the new business is a help or a hindrance for coping with life at home. We've had one or two memorable group meetings at home - especially that Friday when so much booze was consumed it was extraordinary! And we still got a good deal of work done. There's lots of enthusiasm and excitement about.

I wonder what Roy is going to do - perhaps he will get his energy back - is he depressed or ill? - or a bit of both? I wish we knew - it depresses me to see him so sleepy all the time, so vulnerable. I daren't talk about it really as it all makes me want to cry.

Up to this point, we had been dealing with latent, speculative medical problems. Though Roy had clearly not been well, there was nothing particular or identifiable. This was both unnerving and reassuring: unnerving because there was nothing to take hold of and grapple with; reassuring because the absence of illness at least meant things were not immediately grave. This was soon to change.

* * * *

19 May: late: It's two days since Roy was called to the Middlesex after a routine clinic visit. PCP* was diagnosed.

It came as a shock - a gradual, staggering realisation - a terrible fear that he might not come home again. I feel inadequate, uncertain, not knowing how to cope - feeling the awful tension of wanting to be with him and needing to keep hold of house, business, work. I've been disoriented and slightly panicky these last two days (off work Friday) unable to concentrate on customers, restless in the hospital. We've had only short periods together - constant stream of visitors means sociability not intimacy. But the friends are so important - generous, kindly people and so many more on the phone who care about him so much.

When I got back from the hospital on Thursday, Tim held me in his arms while I wept. I've been near to tears

* Starred medical terms like this appear in the glossary on pages 283-287

several times - grieving already for the possible trouble to come.

Roy remains apparently blooming with health - ruddy complexion, cheerful, positive. It's very hard to feel that he's ill at all. Yet this first symptom of the weakness of his defences is terrifying.

After discussion with Roy and his sister, I phoned his mother in Rotherham and told her virtually the whole story - she already suspected - and her reaction was, overall, remarkable - though she said things about how he should never have left home and 'messed about with blokes' and the pain of having children, and so on. But she related things to a wider sphere of reference - we talked about every age having a demon disease - cancer, polio and so on (her sister had had polio) - and how they soon become less terrifying. AIDS will recede in the public consciousness. She talked of his 'going home to be looked after'. I made it clear that this was his home - the place he'd done so much to create and make homely and that he'd be staying here. I said, 'He is not dying.' She was relieved. She was relieved and grateful for the whole communication, I think, though I doubt if she'll sleep much tonight.

I find it difficult to make sense of my feelings - am I denying the reality or over-dramatising it? How serious is the situation really? I've wondered from time to time if I can carry on at all - will the old brain manage all this chaos at once - finishing at the old agency, organising this major exhibition, and a new business, dealing with the staggering change in domestic life - Roy's mum and all - and can I (should I?) keep all this going and risk neglecting Roy or not dealing, really dealing with the feelings and needs of us both? I think that it's right and best to keep hold of the practical, business world - to keep hold of that - if nothing else to ensure that we have an income. But I mustn't get absorbed in it, escape into it and neglect Roy and us.

And now it looks as though the new premises for the business are going to fall through! But everything else is going brilliantly - exhilaratingly! Wow! What a world of extremes.

After the months of preparation, The Bruce Hugman Partnership Ltd, trading as EQUUS, opened its doors on 1 June.

On our checklist of things to be done while there was time, a trip on Concorde featured as a high priority. So we booked one of those round-trips from Heathrow over the Bay of Biscay.

* * * *

2 June: Ninety minutes on Concorde. It delivered everything we could have wished for.

The previous day Roy had been out and about with Mike - all over town, trains buses here and there - and was, early on, obviously tired as we made our way to Heathrow. It was a lovely bright day, with a blue sky dotted with cotton wool clouds. I was full of anticipation.

Check-in was very friendly and welcoming, then we pottered about - had tea and coffee - and waited for announcements. Eventually made our way to gate 50 where there were the remains of a simple, but nicely presented buffet - orange juice and rather small sandwiches. Not quite what we had expected, but we held disappointment at bay.

We listened to an interesting talk about supersonic flight, sonic booms, and the unlikelihood of a replacement for Concorde. We were given our plastic model Concordes.

Packed buses out to the tarmac - and there she was, looking fresh and gleaming. What a wonder!

All very relaxed - no one shoving or pushing - and we were quickly seated in the wide, comfortable grey leather seats. From this moment everything lived up to hopes. Great sense of ease and space inside (though tiny in comparison with conventional aircraft) and lots of very friendly staff buzzing about.

First stage - hot flannels to freshen up, then safety information, lots of chat about the plane, wallet in seats with Supersonic Flyer certificate (collected up and signed by Captain) and other bumph, then lunch menu given out - huge, eight page stylish article - announcing champagne, fillet beef and lots more - very promising!

Take-off was very fast - pressed deep back into seats, Heathrow tearing past outside - afterburn on for 43 seconds from start, then throttle back and out towards Reading.

Display on bulkhead gave speed and height - climbing at a great rate - eventually to 56,000 feet and Mach 2, with the upper cloud cover below us and the darkness of the outer atmosphere above.

Hardly any sensation on passing through sound barrier - just slight thrust as afterburners were engaged for climb and Mach 2.

Lunch looked - and was - quite excellent - mango/fig/melon starter; fillet beef, chicken and pleasant salad; cheese and biscuits; Concorde chocs in little box-and endless champagne - Taittinger and Lanson coming round actually faster than we could drink it!

The sense of ease, luxury and indulgence as we cruised eleven miles up was terrific - a full realisation of all we could have wished. It lasted long enough - there was no feeling that we needed more - it had been complete. A great experience!

In a euphoric mood, and keen to prolong it, we went to the rather rough bar in Terminal 1 and had a bottle of Mercier. We sat and watched the people and enjoyed a great afterglow

2 June Concorde (Roy's entry): Big day, felt really knackered early on. Felt better for a glass of champers. Wonderful day. Hospital in evening - had kebab - very nice - cried myself to sleep - no particular reason, didn't get up till 6pm Sunday. Back in bed at 11 and slept well.

Monday met Miss Lodge 4pm at hospital - had cheesecake, ice cream and coffee - cheesecake very nice but stuck our mouths up - had very nice jolly evening at Albert Hall - 'Opera Spectacular'.

Thursday last day on Pentamadine, thank god, getting too laborious. Manda sat with me five hours till I'd seen the doctor - bless her. Felt irritable - bucked up, had chicken etc. for tea.

'Miss Lodge' was a very dear friend with whom Roy individually and the two of us together had a warm and

indulgent friendship. She had the most wonderful singing voice and a great love of opera. At times she could display a theatricality which would not have disgraced Covent Garden. She always dressed elegantly, often with her hair taken tightly back from her forehead with a bun at the back, in the Spanish fashion. Roy loved her poise and energy. He and she would have extravagant evenings of dressing up and vulgarity and high camp - usually in my absence. Though I knew the kinds of things they got up to, it was actually not till long after his death that Sue showed me photos of some of their more exuberant and surprising evenings.

Manda, Roy's niece - his sister's eldest child - was in her teens at this time. She was also a vivid and colourful personality. Enormously overweight, she dressed brightly and sensibly and was a great bundle of good humour and affection. She and Roy were very close. She was always generous, attentive and relaxed. Like Vera - Roy's Mum - she had a broad, ironic, observant sense of humour, and an eye for the ridiculous, deeply rooted in the stoic culture and language of South Yorkshire.

Pentamadine was the drug prescribed to treat and prevent PCP. It was taken through a nebuliser - a gadget consisting of a face mask attached via an ampoule of the drug to an oxygen cylinder. The pressure of the oxygen nebulised the drug which was then inhaled. Roy found it wearisome rather than unpleasant.

* * * *

3 June: So much is happening so quickly it's almost impossible to keep track, to rest, to deal with it all. I have

recently wondered if I would survive the astonishing pressures - especially in relation to sorting out leaving the agency, the million details, negotiations, discussions and so on which the new business demands. Today (Sunday) I feel a bit panic-stricken by the overwhelming demands of the business - particularly the need for me to provide the drive and initiative and inspiration to get things thoroughly moving. There's so much to do - and no phones, fax or computers or printers to do it all with. Things will fall into place, I'm sure, but the requirements are tremendous.

After his first week in hospital, Roy was discharged, to come home and go in for daily treatment. I think he quite enjoyed hospital - so much attention, care, reassurance, to say nothing of the startling social life! Being at home is much more strenuous - making decisions, structuring the day, travelling into town and so on. And there aren't people around to talk, comfort and pass the time.

He seems to have been in good spirits, seems with his great good sense and stability to be living with and dealing with HIV as well as any man could - we've talked a little - I don't think he's haunted by it now as in the early days - he wants to go back to work if possible - though we've talked about the option of medical retirement. Oh, it's so unfair! How can I make up for it, help him make the most of life and energy? I do feel pretty useless.

They gave him the option of stopping treatment for the PCP after fourteen days, but he chose to go on for twenty-one, and he's got another fourteen-day sick note. He was talking about convalescence at the Lighthouse - sounds an excellent idea in due course perhaps - and another of the really good resources available - all reassuring.

He remains calm and good-tempered, though these two last days have left him washed out - snoozing in bed, operating the video with the stick he calls his remote control.

The Lighthouse was one of the remarkable gay-driven organisations which had sprung up in response to AIDS. The most prominent was The Terence Higgins Trust - named after the first gay man known to have died of AIDS-related illness in the UK. All over the world - especially in America and the UK - there was a huge groundswell of concern and activity, a coming-together of commitment and determination in the face of official indifference or sluggishness. Support groups, information networks, convalescent homes, hospices, publications, research activity - often driven by campaigning, heroic gay men sprung up everywhere. Organisations which pre-dated AIDS - like Gay Switchboard in Britain - quickly adapted their services to take account of the new needs for information and help.

The Lighthouse was one of the real beacons in Britain: a place where the sick and the dying could go for love, attention and nursing care. Founded on the values and principles of the hospice movement, it was a place where gay men could be cared for by those who shared and understood the nature of oppression. It was one of the aspects of the larger world which gave us hope and comfort - and a sense of real pride.

By now, Roy had been promoted and carried responsibility, as Security Supervisor, for the wellbeing of the whole range of London Transport's central sites, duties he took very seriously.

* * * *

23 June: Things were so good that he decided to go back to work - I admire his determination because he could easily have chosen to have more time off - hospital offered sick note and support. He is getting very lethargic at home - whole days in bed feeling weary - cheerful but unable to move!

First week back he's really been in good physical form - though feeling some strain - and he completely overdid it on Tuesday (I think) when he zoomed round all his sites, putting in an appearance, getting up to date. He was very tired on Thursday - and feeling very delicate. Friday evening we met up with friends at Gordon's wine bar in Charing Cross and though he felt tired at one point, the two of us left and went for a delicious Indian meal in Clapham. Roy had a glass and a half of wine at the wine bar then a pint of lager with the meal. It was a very agreeable evening especially as we'd not been out together for a meal for a good while.

Roy had a wonderful evening out at the Albert Hall with Sue and has been playing the CD ever since - 'Opera Spectacular'. The Anvil Chorus has become a kind of theme-tune for him. Such ebullience, such vulgarity!

I've missed going to the clinic with him because of several work commitments and also missed the hospital visit yesterday when he went for his pre-AZT blood sample. It sounds as though it was horrible - lots of attempts to get blood and lots of failures - he was obviously at the limits of endurance. Sample taken eventually.

Seems they're going to monitor him carefully to see effects of AZT* - evidently kindly, patient research nurse explained it all - and gave option not to take part. Roy feels it's a good idea to agree (in spite of prospect of more samples - every fourteen days) and he's pleased to help to find out more - and feels that he may be monitored more closely if he's part of an evaluation.

A Channel 4 Dispatches programme - which we didn't see - has caused great turmoil in the medical world - and for Roy for a few days. He'd almost got to the point of refusing AZT because of it, but there doesn't seem much doubt it was an unbalanced, unreliable study which presented a quite inaccurate picture. Everyone at the hospital was furious about it according to Roy.

Anyway, Wednesday, he got the prescription for AZT and yesterday got a month's supply - 250mg four times a day.

We must try to record accurately how he's been recently to compare with any change. Delicate/queasy stomach from time to time and feeling 'ropey' every two or three days - but seemingly quick recovery next day. Definitely prone to bouts of extreme tiredness even during good days - but sometimes (like yesterday) able to keep going without sleep well into the evening. Tendency to go to bed earlyish - 9 to 10pm - very tired, and seems to be sleeping generally well - some nights frequent waking - but (I think) few sweats recently. I'll leave a space here for his comments.

24 June Roy's entry: You would! Wednesday - saw doctor - she gave me prescription for AZT and told me not to take it until Friday after seeing research nurse - he was a nice chap willing to discuss any questions I asked -

chat for about an hour, then came taking blood - what a performance - me freaking out he couldn't find blood. Eventually other nurse came to do it - my arms were like pin cushions - and felt toothachyish - fancy going through that every fourteen days, but I guess I'll be more closely monitored - also on Wednesday went for Pentamadine only ten minutes. All nurses good but lot of new faces.

Last week had blood taken, had X-ray and blood for oxygen count - everything appears alright but still having coughing fits. Started AZT on Saturday - was quite a step - the only hope but not really wanting to poison my bloodstream - but then it could be said it already is poisoned so we will fight fire with fire.

Spent nearly all weekend gardening and made spaghetti bolognese - sauce very nice.

At this time, AZT was the principal anti-viral drug in use against HIV. Its use was controversial both because of it potential violent and damaging side-effects and because of mixed evidence about its therapeutic effectiveness. Treatment was really still experimental and there were few choices.

24 June: The first day of AZT seems very significant - it's the big chemical gun to add to Roy's psychological armoury at a time when he seems to be in reasonable form. Let's hope it brings back more energy and a greater sense of wellbeing.

What has been strange has been living with this dramatic truth - but both of us carrying on with life - not as if there was nothing wrong, because we do talk about it, but not

letting it get us down or stop us living. Patterns of domestic
life have changed - the balance of responsibility between us
has shifted a little, I think. With very few exceptions (Friday
morning was one) there have been few times of ill-will or
disagreement and generally positive feeling and affection.

30 June Roy's entry: Not been a bad week at work but
there have been several mornings it's taken a while to get
going and been sleeping like a log.

Been on AZT a week now - no serious side-effects but
did have a throbbing headache on Tuesday which won't go
away in spite of painkillers - don't think this warm muggy
weather helps. Going to Flamenco dancing tonight at
Sadler's Wells.

1 July Roy's entry: Woke in a strange mood this morning.
Feeling quite bright but sombre somehow - don't quite
know what to write - feelings and visions keep floating
through but I never have a chance to latch onto them -
they seem to evade me - I want to get pissed and have a fag
and a party but I want to be left alone and get pissed and
cry! See I'm choking up now - should I have a drink - it's
only - oh, it's later than I thought - it's 11:30 so I may
have one - it's now 12:30. Went to feed the birds and
ended up cleaning them out, cooking lamb and sorting
kitchen out in general. Now on my second glass of wine
and feeling a bit better, starting to think about other
things, other than the possible bumpy path that may lie
ahead. Weather has similar feel today as it had in Scotland
- wind strong - whistling up chimney and letterbox and

rattling windows and rain and sunshine. All that's needed now are a few passing joints of venison and it would be complete!

27 August: At home we've hardly had time to stop and notice time flying by. In general Roy has been in very good form - at times, he says, feeling better than ever before - quite wonderful, but then he wondered if AZT were burning him out - but no real sign of that. He's had one or two 'eruptions' (a kind of heat rash and some other oddity) which turned out to be nothing to do with HIV (as far as anyone can tell).

Relations at home have been good (except one night I worked very late at the office and he was cross). We've had some excellent times in London and, especially, on our short hols in Northumberland.

Our determination to make use of our time has been amply fulfilled - we've hardly a free weekend and are booking into November!

There have been times of anxiety - what next? - and Roy has been very shocked by news of the death of two or three from the ward - and of Paul's decline. I haven't seen much of what that has done to his imagination and peace of mind.

He's been much less tired - even through the heat - and on some days has set a pace I've found exhausting. I think it's actually been a very good time for us both - though I've been very tired for much of it with ten or twelve hour days at work, often with things to do on Sundays too. We seem to be doing OK.

16 September: Something of a crisis has been reached: 'I've come to the end of my tether; it's like being in quicksand - clutching at branches; the more you struggle the worse it is.' A grim night. We have to find something active and purposeful.

20 October: Late evening this Saturday, and Roy is in hospital. He has been having sweats again recently, and for some days a persistent, evidently debilitating headache. He has been weary and washed out in the evenings and today looked so helpless on the sofa that I thought he was just giving in. Persuaded him to let me phone the hospital - they invited him in and kept him there for tests and observation. I don't think he's fighting any more.

There have been delightful, good times (even though he's tired quickly) - in Berwick, with friends in Suffolk - but the old spirit's not like it was and he's been so negative, depressive and irritable.

We've had one or two awful days - days of hideous, bitter silence, of relentless, dispiriting aggression; of self-absorption which have excluded and withered me. I have felt his despair? depression? fear? sapping my energy and optimism, draining my vital energies away - and still I've been unable to reach him, to bring him out of it.

Just now his moods - bright or dark - never seem to coincide with mine - when I'm exhausted and drained he's wanting affection and attention; when I'm trying to be bright and attentive he's dark and withdrawn - when he says he wants to hear about what I've been doing I feel he's bored and I stick to family and house; when I tell him about work and the outside world, he's withdrawn and distant.

There was a lovely phone call out of the blue today from an unknown American who'd read the Gay Times piece - he was so enthusiastic about the content and the quality of the writing - I told Roy - his only reaction was one of anxiety that someone had located me. Why did we write it and send it off? he said. To touch the lives of others. And we did.

There have been good times - lovely moments, some of them even - especially? - after the worst times (that has happened to us before) - moments when the horror and stupidity of having rows collapses with the realisation of how seriously things are going wrong.

It seems as though we had a lovely summer - where did it go? - good, happy, harmonious times when his energy was predictable, when there was optimism.

He picked up in hospital - I think he doesn't know how to keep himself going - he needs to be taken in hand - needs to be in a safe place - being on your own at home doesn't provide that - there's too much time to think, too comfortable a sofa to sink into, too much easy mindless distraction on TV - he so often leaves it on even when I come in, keeping me out, at a distance. And I need nourishment and support too.

He gives too - sometimes I come home and there's a meal prepared. He continues to look after the house and garden - sometimes with great energy - but it's all become terribly, damagingly unpredictable. And he blames me for long hours at work, has been sulky and cross when I come in late. There is so much pressure.

And on him, too, of course. I don't know what to do but to be as steady as I can, with occasional lapses. I don't know what to do.

Recently I have felt anxiety about coming home - fear of what I will find; I still love home, love coming home, but there's doubt and anxiety now - will it be easy, relaxed, affectionate or strained and dispiriting?

I do feel sorry for myself. Tired and strained. Yet I must carry on.

He's finding travel more difficult - car or train - and suffers from frequent stomach pain and discomfort. Some mornings he's so weary he can hardly get out of bed - yet he's not missed a day at work and seems to be keeping his commitments fully under control. That's probably why he has so little spare energy at home.

In other years, I could, perhaps have given up work - we could have spent more good time together - but could we be content without our home, our life without cash to spend? I doubt it. And the penalty for meeting those needs is going out to work. And now, for me, with much more dramatic and demanding responsibility - the business has to be a success, and it can't function without me, not for years.

Once more, he is in the best hands - and anything must be better than the sad state he's been in recently - even with the occasional ups. Let's hope for some good weeks ahead.

11 November 9:15pm: I've just waved him off in the cab back to the hospital, after his thirty hours or so at home.

These are the hard times.

He's so far from well, yet they can find nothing major. Poor Roy, he's been like a laboratory specimen these past weeks - every test known to medical science, endless blood samples (how he hates needles) - how brave he has been as he's been punctured and prodded and invaded.

I've just broken off writing to phone the hospital - talked to the sister who described him as a 'beautiful' patient - and arranged to talk to the consultant tomorrow - perhaps he can help us out of this awful uncertainty.

Not knowing - not knowing what's wrong; not knowing how long it will last; not knowing if he'll get better; not knowing if he'll be his old, energetic, jovial self again; not knowing if he'll always be a patient at home now.

I'm becoming depressed, as he is, at this uncertain future, this painful present.

The quality of medical care we found, and the astonishing quality of the people at the clinic and in the ward amazed us. All our fantasies about hostile sisters were banished from the very beginning.

We learnt what a radical effect the admission of AIDS patients had had upon ward culture: here were vigorous, articulate, almost exclusively young men who insisted on information, choice, collaboration. They wanted to know what lay behind treatment options, what the risks and benefits were; they were not willing to wake up graciously at absurd hours to have their breakfast and their temperatures taken; they were not willing to submit to whatever the Great God Consultant said was good for them. They were determined to make their own informed choices.

All this, of course, should have been par for the course - for any patient, with any illness, in any ward. But it wasn't, and sadly still isn't the case.

What we found were doctors and nurses who deeply and completely accepted their patients as partners in the therapeutic experiment. In those days, of course, it was even more of an experiment than it is now, and those we knew had the realism and humility to acknowledge that there was very little certainty in anything they did. They were learning as they went along and we were grateful that we were included in the process. What we had to say and what we experienced were part of the advancement of science. It made us feel valuable beyond our ordinary value as human beings, which itself was so conspicuously recognised.

The use of 'we' is entirely accurate. While Roy was the patient, there was no time at which that identity superceded his individual rights or human dignity, and no time at which it was not acknowledged that his identity, needs and wishes arose also essentially from our partnership. So, at any time at all, and particularly at crucial times, I was treated as his equal in terms of access to information, participation in decisions, assertion of what we wanted. They understood what we had yet to learn: Roy's morale and wellbeing, and even his health to a real extent, were dependent on the strength and health of our relationship, and on the welfare of both of us individually.

There was, in many respects, a sense of normality about the ward. Perhaps I should say extraordinary normality, because it was a place of humour, kindness, informality, idiosyncrasy, devotion and creativity, where the medicine felt subsidiary to the human relations. Any occasion for celebration and decoration

*was seized upon: all the usual festive occasions - Christmas,
Easter, birthdays and so on - but also Beaujolais Nouveau
Day, Guy Fawkes' night, the annual ward party and much
more. There was a sense of vigour and life and optimism about
the place. People died on the ward, but they died in an embrace
of rare and genuine love.*

* * * *

17 November (written on the train en route home from
Newcastle): Roy has been in hospital just four weeks now.
For three and a half weeks it was tests - day after day -
blood tests, bone marrow, lumbar puncture, liver biopsy -
such an assault on his frail, feverish body. They found
nothing which could explain the fever, sweats, lethargy.
White cells had fallen seriously so AZT was stopped -
within a week white cells recovered. They decided to give
antibiotics in the hope that whatever it was causing the
problems would be knocked out. First day and a half of
antibiotics (hefty doses intravenously) he was very sluggish
and high - third day woke up feeling better; fourth (today)
tired - but fevers and sweats have stopped - but he is
breathless just moving his position in bed.

Yesterday I had the day off and spent a few hours with him
- bathed him, sat, talked - there was really no pressure on
time and it was very agreeable. I had been feeling so much
pressure, so many things to do, so much dashing around.

This journey - a packed Saturday afternoon train - is a
nightmare - I feel hemmed in, restricted, stressed. Wish I'd
taken the Weekend First option - open spaces, decent seats -
but couldn't smoke.

Our hope and objective at the moment is that he will be well for Christmas and that we can have a few days of peace and quiet together at home.

He fears the prospect of further illness and going through all this horror again.

I really don't know how to survive the pressures of work and visiting, Christmas cards and presents, washing - just keeping going. I leave the house 6:30am - return 9ish after work and hospital, if I'm lucky. It's wearing me down!

But what of his poor body? Can it survive this radical assault both from the virus and the treatment (which isn't at present nearly as radical as it might be)?

He's eaten hardly anything for three weeks (had a bite or two of a burger today and a milkshake) - will he start losing weight? Friends have been very good.

He is so far from being himself.

18 November: I have just returned home from two days' work in Newcastle - and a visit to the hospital where I went straight from the train. Our talk to the consultant lifted the deepest strands of the depression - at least we were coming to the end of 'testing' - but they did not have any idea what was wrong (except very low white cells - hence AZT stopped last week, and low haemoglobin). They were going to start broad spectrum antibiotics in the hope they'd blast whatever the bug was.

They've been pouring the stuff into his veins for three days now and he's no better. The sweats have stopped (except late last night when painkillers provoked a real torrent and his temperature plummeted - they used a foil heat-conservation blanket they were so alarmed). But he's so weary and now (again) depressed.

Had a chat with night staff nurse tonight - such wisdom and strength and concern (he's been wonderful to Roy over this period) - he thought Roy needed to cry - so much bottled up; he thought there was no more I could do than continue to love him; he offered the ward's camp bed for me to stay overnight in Roy's room. I decided to go home.

I thanked him for his care and affection - expressed again our confidence in the team - their affection, their commitment.

(They had Beaujolais Nouveau and peanuts rattling round on a medical trolley on the ward the other day - they don't miss any opportunity to bring life and entertainment to the place!)

I realise I'd been feeling insecure financially recently - what happens if I'm ill? - can we keep the house on? The business is a risk - there's no comfortable safety net beneath us - we've no wealth behind us - only our deaths will make us rich!

I don't know where we're going.

Tonight we talked of having a quiet Christmas here at home together - that would be wonderful - I hope it's something Roy can pin his hopes on and work towards - he seems so helpless, vulnerable there in his bed - nothing to occupy his mind except his illness.

He had a few bites of a hamburger tonight - but very slight signs of a revival of interest in food.

15 December: He has been home for two weeks now and the improvement in his health and energy has been astonishing. Only three weeks ago in hospital, just walking down the ward was a trial - bathing an agonising, anxious business. Now he's going shopping, pottering about the house - at this minute cooking bacon and egg and fried bread!

We lived on a kind of roller-coaster of highs and lows in health and emotion: from one day to the next it was impossible to anticipate how well Roy would be and where on the spectrum of apparently near-death to exuberant energy we would find his poor body. While our emotions were largely tied to the immediate state of his health each hour and each day, there were also other quite different currents sweeping through us with their own unpredictable and powerful rhythms. These rose from the very deepest aspects of our being, associated with life and death, meaning and purpose of life, the moral emptiness of the universe and all those dark, unknowable fears which live on the edge of existence, and rise up in the wake of crisis.

While the dark times were as dark as anything I ever expect to experience, the bright times were exquisite just because they were at the polar opposite to the previous despair. We had never espoused the middle path, but we had never imagined that such extremities were available either side of it.

Christmas was one of the blissful periods of health, peace and quiet time together. With just the two of us on Christmas Day, we mounted the whole show - stockings, opening presents in bed; full-scale dinner with elaborate table-setting, candles, silver, fine linen; goose and trimmings - the whole shebang. And the house, as always when Roy was in charge, was festooned with Christmas lights - dozens of sets round every doorway, along every picture rail, round every picture and three or four on the enormous tree - weighed down with his usual dozens and dozens of colourful glass balls. The team was back in action!

* * * *

6 January 1991: The general improvement in his health has continued and he returned to work at the beginning of the month. It does not seem to have been too difficult, though he's tired at the end of the day. He's anxious about the possible implications of his employer finding out about his illness.

I'm not very clear how he's feeling at the deeper levels - he says things have been entirely changed for him - at times he clearly (and reasonably!) feels sorry for himself; at others seems happy simply to carry on 'as normal'.

We had a long talk the other night when he said, amongst other things, that he was 'happy with his lot' - meaning, I think, with our home, our life, how we spend our time, the sense we're managing to make of the inevitable.

We talked about the financial implications of his stopping work. I felt that we could manage tolerably well - especially if the business prospers and my salary increases substantially at the year end. Things will be tighter, but we have been throwing money around fairly liberally!

Since restarting AZT he's been feeling better, though there have been some night sweats and headaches. The indigestion (or whatever) recurs occasionally but doesn't seem too serious. He's still moving about quite slowly and finds stairs a problem at work and home.

With the exception of one incident, we had an almost perfect Christmas break. I had the full ten days off. For the first six days we really did more or less exactly what we pleased - sleeping late, eating, shopping, snoozing, having friends round for drinks, but largely having the time just to ourselves. It was very affectionate and harmonious - a very happy time indeed. Christmas lunch with our free range goose was excellent and it was wonderful just being able to please ourselves.

The only cloud over Christmas - and it was a pretty dark one - was the phone call from his sister on Christmas morning which knocked Roy for six and sent me into a fury of indignation - which I vented fully on the phone to her later in the day. She rang to accuse Roy of selfish disregard for his Mum on the one day in the year when families should stick together. She was in a dark and vicious mood. Roy came back from the phone depressed and dispirited. I brooded on this nasty intrusion for several days and was in no frame of mind to go north and see her and the rest of Roy's family as we had planned.

The trip to Roy's Mum in Rotherham was fine - no nasties or problems - lots of good food, fairly relaxed time, a shopping trip to Meadowhall. Normal - if cool - relations resumed with his sister and no references to the Christmas outrage.

Good time at my parents where we were treated to lots of grub and drink - warmly welcomed. It was great to see my brother and sister-in-law and the two very attractive, civilised nephews.

Before Christmas we went to the ward party which was a remarkable event - the room packed with staff and current and ex-patients all on a serious extravagant binge. There was cabaret - wonderfully tacky and camp with one of the male nurses in a frock and wig and others being very amusing. The whole experience was weird - those excellent nurses letting their hair down - those who had played such a vital part in the health of the party-goers (many of them very ill) and who had given affection and hope so generously.

We presented the ward with a four foot cuddly bear in hat and scarf which remained in the day-room for months afterwards.

The Christmas phone call caused me real fury and turmoil. It touched all kinds of old conflicts and pains. While I had had a very secure and pretty privileged childhood, I had rarely been happy at home. Certainly as I entered puberty and felt the power of my sexuality assert itself, I was deeply uneasy and unsettled. I was equally irritated by my seemingly obsessive mother and apparently passive, diffident father.

Once I went away to University and started work, I found it increasingly difficult to spend more than a few hours at home without becoming irritable and depressed. Leaving home and setting up my own independent existence became something of a crusade including, of course, resisting the usual duty calls of family life such as going home for Christmas.

'Home' was to be where one's life was centred. It had the extra dimension that, as a gay man, I could not establish the kind of home that most people would take seriously: could there be a home without a wife and children? Well, yes, there could and I was determined to demonstrate how.

Breaking those ties, offending against the constant external and internal iteration of filial and family obligations is a major challenge. In time I achieved what I wanted: where I lived was the centre of my existence with all the depth and weight of 'home'. This meant spending Christmas there with those I chose and who chose me - among my 'pseudo-family' as it was satirically described by one of the witches of the century.

I had achieved this transition before I met Roy. After his initial doubts about leaving Rotherham (which were actually more about declaring his sexuality than leaving), we built two homes together which were absolutely all I could have dreamed of - and which he felt the power of as much as I. But these things are not achieved without struggle against the overwhelming values of so-called normal family life and against the sometimes stentorian claims of those who feel side-lined or neglected - or those who represent such claims through their own frustration and disappointment.

Even Vera, for all her wisdom and strength, found it difficult to comprehend that the home in which Roy would want to be looked after would not be hers. It was as if she saw our years together as a kind of transient interlude which would end with a return to real life.

Roy's achievement was considerable simply because he had been and remained to the end so very close to Vera, even though he never declared or discussed his sexuality with her. I think I was jealous and insecure about his ties with her in the early days, but as our relationship matured so did my willing acceptance of the crucial nature of his relationship with her.

How complicated all this is! I remember Roy and I had one or two conversations about having children. He once declared himself to be feeling 'broody'. He had such reservoirs of love. Our world was almost exclusively adult. For him that did not in the least mean a world without love, but a world in which the uninhibited expression of love was difficult, though he loved and was loved extravagantly.

While he was furious and depressed after the phone call - and did not forget it - like so many things, he let it pass and, as far as I know, did not mention it to his mother or confront his sister.

* * * *

10 January: In general, things have been going well. Roy has been gaining strength day by day and now carries out a day's work with no more difficulty or weariness than previously.

There was some concern about a drop in his T-cell count (very minor) and he's now on a half dose of AZT. Minor sinus problems emerged and most recently he's had a horribly painful mouth infection (candidiasis) which gives him no peace and makes eating a grim business. Other than those minor problems he has been well and in good spirits - which has been wonderful to see after the grim weeks before Christmas.

In terms of social life we've been pretty busy. We had an excellent, excessive evening with friends at Le Café des Amis Du Vin. My birthday was excellent - cabaret at the Drill Hall, followed by nightclub and an early morning night-bus home (just like old times!) and lunch with Mark on my birthday - which was lengthy, excessive and very enjoyable.

We went to see the cabaret for a second time and then on another evening struggled through the awful weather and the collapsing transport to Greenwich to see Patricia Routledge in The Corn is Green.

6 April: It is Saturday evening of a free weekend; I have just finished a zip through the study sorting out the ever accumulating junk, and throwing out a good deal of stuff. Roy's snoozing in the front room.

The great event since the last entry was our trip to California. Apart from Roy enduring a horrific cough, it was most successful and we had a very good time.

Without rushing about, we did a good deal - in San Diego a trip to Mexico; a long bus ride up the coast to Ocean Beach (and a stroll along the pier; refreshments at a 'Dairy Queen'; the strange slightly uneasy feel in the town - odd characters wandering about or slouching on street corners); whale-watching trip (dolphins but no whales); sightseeing on the 'old trolley'; organ concert in Balboa Park and a visit to the Zoo (we saw a confrontation between demonstrators and Mounted Police in the park);

several delightful meals (Seaport Village mostly, though Roy wasn't very hungry most of the time); sickly fudge; shopping; champagne in our room; breakfast brought by Jesus (to our delight!)

In San Francisco we did a great sightseeing trip with an eccentric and enthusiastic coach driver; visited Alcatraz; spent some time in Castro; rode endlessly on the cable cars and went to the cable house museum; shopped and ate; I saw Hamlet at the American Conservatory Theatre; Roy quickly acquired a taste for oysters and champagne; we drank in a lively and friendly bar; went to Macey's (what a store - four floors of men's clothes!) and ate huge and delicious meals in TGI Fridays (where, on one occasion, we had our only row).

It was excellent - excellent to have travelled that far, to have been to The States, to have got sunburnt in March, to have crossed the Atlantic at last - and to discover we'd earned enough frequent flyer miles to go back for nothing!

At home we've been to see The Trackers of Oxyrynchus at the National Theatre (and again next week we liked it so much); delicious Wind in the Willows (with my brother and sister-in-law and nephews); went with friend to see Buddy - tacky second-rate show; Roy went home for Easter and I stayed quietly here - reading and writing.

There have been no great dramas - Roy's cough has been a worry (and a pain for him) but it seems to be nothing too serious and is clearing up; the latest on his cell count is good news, though he does seem a bit off-colour and nauseous from time to time. His doctor at the clinic remains a great joy - friendly, straightforward, committed.

It looks as though Roy's job is going to change a good deal as he changes departments - more work and demands, but more contact with people and more stimulation. He's been very bored with the job up to now - it may be a good change all round.

Five months of life as nearly normal as we could hope for, and so very much better than we might have feared. But the rollercoaster was about to take one of its precipitous plunges from which we couldn't be sure we'd rise again.

* * * *

12 May: Roy's health now becomes our great preoccupation. Last Thursday we learnt he has CMV Retinitis* in his right eye and needs intensive chemo-therapy to keep it at bay - daily for three weeks, then five days a week maintenance. He'll now need a Hickman line* inserted.

Immediately after the examination on Thursday, he went to the ward for his first Ganciclovir*. He was very late back - I was in Newcastle and also very late - (I always seem to be away on the big days). I talked to his doctor on Friday - we really didn't know much about it. I asked her how long this might mean he'd got. And the news was not comforting. There are some of her patients with CMV who've survived thirty months - but average less, possibly twelve.

Friday we went to the ward together and the consultant fitted a long line into his vein to avoid the necessity for daily injections - almost entirely painlessly, real artistry (what a relief for Roy!) and he had his second dose of

Ganciclovir. News about the Hickman line and the independence it gives seemed good - the consultant talked of globe-trotters calling in to the ward from all over the world to have adjustments made to their Hickman lines!

Saturday (yesterday) we had a good day - leisurely breakfast, journey to Waterloo - coffee and cakes - Carmen Jones at the Old Vic (great show - me a bit weepy at sentimental bits) then onto the ward, where they had Roy's drugs prepared and were their usual sweet, welcoming selves.

We then went off to the Spaghetti House and ate and drank well. Very straight talk about the situation. Roy said he felt time was running out - how he dreaded an up escalator not working, how the digging to put the (neglected) Dutch tulips in had exhausted him - how much of a trial the journey to work was - waiting for trains on which he would be sure of a seat - taking lifts to the first floor.

We talked seriously of our trip round the world - a boat up the Nile, the rainforests, Hawaii, possibly in November, but on Sunday both thought we should do it sooner - Roy must be well enough to enjoy it.

We have to guard against feelings that 'it's all over'. It certainly isn't and there may be years yet - though Roy doesn't feel there will be. He said how he feels his energy is going - that his weight isn't 'real' solid weight - that he could go downhill.

It's difficult to take it all in. I was feeling some degree of shock on Friday - abstracted moments, risk of losing concentration and still feel that I've not got to grips with things - how do we make the best use of our time? How do we come to terms with the uncertain timescale?

Roy has shown his usual strength and humour through all this - when told that the CMV infection looked like a 'pizza' on his retina he asked if there were anchovies on it; we've discussed the new, blockbusting, detective mystery, Murder on the Hickman Line. He's shown exactly the same practical, tough reaction as ever: get on with it! On the first day, his reaction was - we must get out and see the world while I can. He is amazing. And, he says, I agree, it's not just a matter of attitude, this survival game. It's also a matter of inevitable processes working their way through, though the pace may be determined by attitude.

We had a conversation about collecting the equipment for murder - injecting Weedol into the drip - though we discovered there were much simpler ways!

We haven't decided what he should do about work - we talked about continuing up to the point (but not beyond it) that he can carry out his duties to his employer's satisfaction, then going sick and not returning. We're wondering about how to cope with the Hickman line operation and convalescence - unpaid leave, wisdom tooth extraction?

I don't think he has any regrets about our life. He says he has no great ambitions, and what he's wanted we've done or are planning to do (round the world seems to be the major outstanding thought) - and, as we often comment, compared with many we've done and continue to do a great deal.

It's impossible to imagine life without him, without the almost entirely harmonious life we've had - sharing our home mostly easily and happily, holidays, trips, theatre, entertaining here - we're such an accomplished team at that! I mentioned this last night and he said, 'You'll throw yourself into work' - and I daresay that will be one reaction. I don't at all want to think about it, though it's impossible not to as we come to terms with this latest development.

Oh, it is so sad. Such spirit, such sparkle, loved by so many people!

I'm going to work out how much money we've got available now for our trip.

16 June: What a month of shocks, surprises, pleasures and pressure! Roy was having his Ganciclovir every day - making the day very long - never seemed to take less than four or five hours, and there were lots of hassle with canulas etc. The operation for the Hickman line was arranged very quickly - one week and it was done. The day after he was demanding Kentucky Fried Chicken and on Saturday we went to Five Guys Named Moe - what a wonderful, lively, amusing, catchy show! He was feeling physically very vulnerable, fearing someone bumping into him, as we made slow, cautious progress on foot for the mile or so from the hospital to the theatre.

He was back at work on the following Tuesday - amazingly, and we started learning how to administer the drugs. Very anxious start for us both - me blowing the needle off the syringe once, and pricking my finger another time - but it soon came, once the initial hurdle was over. Much the most unnerving bit was flushing out the line after disconnecting the drip - pushing saline and Heparin* directly into him. It looks as though I shall be the nurse.

That week I went to see the bank manager after writing to him about a loan for our trip. He was very responsive and helpful.

Bank holiday weekend Roy's mum and aunt and uncle came and we had a very relaxed and happy time. Aunt seems to be very tough and well-balanced. She's looking after mum, to some extent - a real comfort for her we felt - and for us to know she has someone to talk to.

A real blow this week: the Ganciclovir doesn't seem to be doing the trick and they want to add Foscarnet*, making many hours of treatment each day. Almost instant admission (how our fortunes change by the hour!) - though Roy wanted to work from hospital, they didn't see any way it could be managed (if there were a way they'd have found it).

We went to Northampton for my parent's Golden Wedding on Sunday and Roy insisted on working the Monday because his boss was away. Agonies about what to say at work - Roy, ingenious and resourceful as ever, planned it all to do least damage (though I don't know what he said).

During this time I was worried that just being in hospital would depress mind and body, but he met Keith from Barnsley on the ward and struck up a great companionship. They call themselves the 'Ganciclovir gang' and were going through much the same treatment at

A perfect partnership (mid-eighties)

Roy with the black rabbit on the day of its emigration from Balham to
Northamptonshire (1991)

the same stage as each other. They sit in a corner of the ward with their drips up, gossiping and laughing. Very Yorkshire.

We had a couple of delightful, spontaneous evenings. One with Mark - came along to the ward for a chat before going back to his prepared supper - but we ended up going out to eat in an attractive bistro near the hospital and ate and drank and had a very happy time. A couple of evenings later Roy and I went out for a drink at the nearest pub to the hospital, and ended up in the pasta house having a great evening - happy, relaxed conversation and good will. How I enjoy these times together!

After the first week, I had to go away to the north-east, but happily Roy had plenty of visitors, expeditions and also went three times as a 'guinea pig' for medical students' exams - no chance of sinking into lethargy! We spoke on the phone once or twice every day.

The speed with which things change is unnerving - the sudden necessity to go into hospital, the feeling that anything could happen, any time.

Negotiations for the bank loan have been successful though rather depressing. We're borrowing more than £20,000 against the security of Roy's life policies. The Bank Manager apologised for having to ask for evidence from the hospital of Roy's relatively short life-expectancy. We were able to deal with all this rather more briskly than he was, poor man! But we've both been anxious, I think, about his being well enough to enjoy the trip.

It's amazing how one adapts - especially how Roy's adapted - to the Hickman line (it is bizarre - this piece of plastic hanging out of his chest), to the necessity of new, troublesome routines, to the perception that something odd is happening to his nails, to the cough - I don't know how he manages to be so stoic, heroic, calm. I asked him today (16/6) how he was feeling emotionally - and he said 'alright' - and I think he is. He's still full of humour too - conversation just, about the internal 'balloon' which stops the Hickman line falling out: Roy: 'I said to Nurse Cathy, with all this flying round the world I hope it doesn't inflate and I come back with inflated left titty!'

I felt great stress during the days after he went into hospital, especially the thought of the long days, the complications, the trudging here and there - not that I didn't want to do whatever was necessary, but could I keep up, could I find the energy?

Things have really been hotting up at work too with lots of substantial and important demands.

Now everything is set for the World Trip and we hold our breath to see if he'll be well enough to go.

Family Occasions
Top Up north for a wedding in Sheffield. Roy's sister and girls with Vera (1991)
Middle At the Deakin family home in Rotherham (1987)
Bottom Bruce's parents' Golden Wedding (1991). Mary and Peter are front row, right

Roy building the avairy at our first London home (1985)

The DIARY

Part II

Round the World - July-August 1991

Within moments of our settling comfortably into the prettily upholstered armchairs at our table for two on the Orient Express at Victoria Station, champagne was being poured for us by the elegantly-uniformed, white-gloved steward, and Roy said: 'I'm so happy I could cry.'

His unreserved pleasure was the sweetest possible gift for me. Not only did his feeling match mine exactly, but with that shared delight there was also a sense of triumph - that we were there at all; that it felt so perfect; that amidst so much uncertainty not the slightest shadow darkened the sunshine of the moment.

On the table was fine bone china, silverware and crisp linen; round us were the rich colours of polished walnut, the gleam of brass and bevelled mirrors; the gentleness of pretty fabrics and soft carpet. We were looking terrific - as we did throughout the trip! - this time in blazers and cravats: all was beautifully well.

Outside the window - already - there seemed to be another, strange world - a world of mid-tones, of diluted

sensations, of uneventfulness: we felt like royalty, suddenly translated from ordinariness to a new and exotic plane. It was a fantasy into which we fell easily enough without encouragement, but it was reinforced by the curious, enraptured spectators whom the train attracted wherever it went: as we pulled out of Victoria - champagne in hand - onlookers waved to us as if we were the famous; at every station people stared with fascination into the cocooned luxury and at the elegant creatures within it.

While sustained luxury, personal attention and the indulgence of every whim were actually extraordinary for us, what was striking was how absolutely natural it felt - that this was, indeed, how things should be, how one could most completely be oneself, how all people should live. And our conversion was instant: it required no adaptation, no negotiation and we felt no guilt. As we lay in that same warm embrace of luxury round the world for a month, the pleasure did not diminish.

The train pulled out of Victoria, and we settled back to a new rhythm - that unique rhythm of care-less travel where all that is to be contemplated is the pleasure of the present - and the glorious succession of days stretching ahead.

* * * *

Our itinerary was to take us to Venice; to Delhi; Agra; Jaipur; Hong Kong; San Francisco; Jamaica; Barbados; and New York, from where we would sail back to England on the QE2. We were to fly first or business class everywhere, and stay in the best hotels - expense was not an issue. We were on the trip of a lifetime and there was to be no prudence.

We had packed two wardrobes - one the informal wear of the tourist in warm places; the other the formal wear of the first class traveller - dinner suits, jackets, tailored shirts and trousers. We had also pretty impressive pharmaceutical luggage - all the gear for twenty Ganciclovir treatments (needles, syringes, 100ml saline, giving sets, sterile sprays and wipes, Heplok flush) and tablets enough to make a customs officer's eyes pop. To our surprise and relief we were not questioned about such compromising freight - except as we left India when the packages were briefly queried before the cases were sealed. We had a wad of authorising documentation, signed and stamped, but we did not relish the prospect of interrogation about the gear nor about the cause of our carrying it.

The Ganciclovir was prescribed to inhibit the progress of the CMV in Roy's already damaged eye and was to be administered five days in seven. The routine had become second nature to us at home, and we quickly adapted to the circumstances of each new location - the drip being hung variously from picture hooks, hat stands, luggage racks or coat hangers on land and at sea. Our meticulous preparations meant we had forgotten nothing and the procedure - with which we had so anxiously fumbled at first - went like quiet clockwork. We had a miniature sharps safe for the storage of used needles but were forced somewhat self-consciously to leave parcels of empty syringes, ampoules, giving sets and other debris in litter bins and baskets round the globe.

Roy was much amused by the name of this hotel

A late lunch in Venice

We had been offered the Intermate alternative to making up the drug for each treatment: this remarkable object is a small plastic capsule (about the size of an elongated tennis ball) in which there is a small bladder containing the appropriate dose of drug in solution, surrounded by a vacuum in the outer capsule. All that is required is connection to the Hickman line and the drug administers itself.

A fortnight's supply (ten doses for us) could be delivered at one time, and we had got as far as finding out that we could pick up a second supply in San Francisco to see us through the second half of the holiday. The problem was that it had to be kept refrigerated and it was that - in spite of the enormous convenience and simplicity of the system - which made us decide against it. No doubt it would have been possible, but it would have been a constant anxiety and constantly have required favours from cabin staff, hotels and so on. Once home, however, we changed over to the system and were very grateful for the simplifying of one element of the day's routines.

Throughout the holiday Roy was plagued intermittently by vomiting, diarrhoea and bouts of coughing and had some miserable nights. It was a small comfort that, usually, after being sick he felt much better for several hours - but our anxiety was that tablets rarely stayed long enough in his body to do much good. Among the dozens of prescribed tablets he became selective about those he felt worth giving even half a chance and, for example, stopped taking the daily and weekly anti-malarials, remarking that the effects of a mosquito bite were rather low on his list of medical preoccupations.

There were times when he was very tired and washed out, but he also recovered very quickly. He found energy from some deep, steely source which kept him master of discomfort and available for pleasure most of the time - and, as became clear - actively postponed serious illness through sheer effort of will.

I too was drawing on reserves of strength which were perfectly focused to our needs, the exercise of which, and their intimate relationship with Roy's morale, I was almost completely unaware of until our short crisis in New York. The administrative and physical demands were substantial: we were leaving and entering new countries every four days or so; every departure and arrival required packing and unpacking of our considerable luggage; there were immigration procedures (entering India with portable CD player, video camera and dictaphone required a conference of thousands, the signatures of most of them and the filling of many pages in heavy ledgers with marbled end-papers); there was currency to be exchanged (for those countries where it was not available in advance); hotel documentation to be completed; and all the details of hotels, countries, cities, money, transport, sights and activities to be swiftly mastered. There were the demands of the medical regime and the simple, profound requirement for me just to keep us on the move, and almost unconsciously to be in constant negotiation with Roy about how he felt, what he wanted, what he could cope with, how far we could push ourselves.

Transport up the hill to the Amber palace - and the 'royal tapestries'

Grand accommodation in Jaipur

I did not really feel any of this at the time. I now think there are extraordinary, unknown aspects of personality which quietly assert themselves in such circumstances - working benignly and constructively to deal with almost whatever demands present themselves: some kind of wonderful reflex which switches on elements of personal strength and frees one from burdens of effort which could otherwise be quite crushing.

Roy exhibited similar strength: he was far from passive or inactive, indeed in his freedom to act and to enjoy he was astonishing. That, in its turn, clearly nourished me.

* * * *

Amidst all this, we had some of the happiest and most companionable times of our already happy and companionable lives: there were quite wonderful occasions when all that existed for us was being together, the mood of harmony, the perfection of the setting, the place, the food - when nothing intruded and life seemed consummated.

Such times could not be contrived - they were part of the rich serendipity of travel matched with our instinct to seize the moment.

A few sketches will convey how it was. The state of relative physical luxury in which we lived for most of the time provided a powerful foundation for a mood of relaxation and well-being. After the Orient Express - with all its style and elegance; the courteous, warm attention of its staff; the lovely food, champagne and flowers; the astonishing Alpine landscape - we were ready for a more stable environment than a train for, in the end, Roy found the constant motion troubling his stomach.

From the railway station in Venice we were taken by water taxi along the Grand Canal, under a pure blue afternoon sky, past the waterfront to St Mark's Square and the Doges' palace, to the Hotel Danielli a few buildings along.

Our spacious, high-ceilinged room, air-conditioned and blissfully cool, was elegantly furnished, with a great, golden chandelier and a vast double bed. The sparkling bathroom was floored and walled in white marble, veined with grey; the piles of fluffy towels and crisp linen sheets were themselves serious pleasures. There were chocolates and fruit awaiting us, fresh flowers, and a refrigerator full of champagne and drinks of all kinds.

Beyond the shuttered windows was a balcony overlooking the lagoon, directly opposite San Giorgio Maggiore, with the Grand Canal and the entrance to St Mark's Square just to the right. It was a glorious, golden summer evening and Venice was alive with all the sights and sounds of people, boats, bells, trade and pleasure; gondolas, vaporetti, pleasure cruisers and craft of all imaginable kinds were busily crisscrossing the lagoon and beneath us on the waterfront hundreds of people strolled and talked and bartered and laughed.

That evening we had oysters and champagne in a restaurant of supreme style and startling expense.

After a relatively peaceful night we were woken by the arrival of breakfast on two enormous trays. Roy had a sweet, cool melon - the size of half a football - filled with raspberries, strawberries and blackberries; soft scrambled

Stanley Market, Hong Kong

Relaxing in Barbados

egg; fresh-squeezed lemon juice (the sharpest known to man, we remarked); tea and a mountain of fresh rolls and sweet pastries. I had fruit salad, coffee and croissants, marvelling, like him, at the layers of crisp linen, the huge napkins, the silver and the china: the sheer joy of it!

Slowly we finished, did the first Ganciclovir routine of the holiday, showered, dressed and went out to explore in the bright, sharp heat of the late morning.

We walked a little, took vaporetti here and there, explored churches, wandered along little canals, bought a Panama to protect my balding head from the sun, stood on the Rialto amidst the hubbub of tourist Venice, and then sought refreshing drinks. We went into a restaurant, indicating our wish only to drink, and were brought tea and beer. The waiter wondered if we might not like to eat something and told us he had a turbot - the last of the day - which would be just perfect for two.

The next two hours passed in a timeless haze of amiable conversation, turbot, vegetables, fruit salads and ice cream, white wine, coffees and several of the largest glasses of grappa I have ever seen. Having not initially felt at all hungry we were affectionately satirical about our capacity to be seduced by any indulgence that presented itself, and resumed our amble in the sunshine.

In one of the churches we visited, I was moved to light a candle for Roy, and he lit one for his mother - gestures, I think, of a kind of pagan romanticism, quite untypical of two thoroughly unreligious chaps and certainly not intended to propitiate priests, saints or other holy beings. Our home was always full of candles and, here in this new world, there was something sweetly moving about lighting a flame and leaving it burning in so ancient, gloomy and evocative a place.

In the end, we got lost, walked far too much, and Roy was exhausted and frail by the time we arrived back at the hotel in the late afternoon. We both slept long and deep until after seven.

We showered (the mass of huge, fluffy towels had been replaced since the morning), and set out to explore in the gentler temperatures of the fading evening light.

Yet again we found ourselves being tempted to a table, this time by a handsome young Italian whose sales-talk and smile were irresistible. After shrimps with oil and lemon juice, entrecôte, seabass with crayfish, wine, gateau, coffee and more grappa, watching the hundreds of passers-by, we strolled along the waterfront, enjoying that simplest of pleasures - observing the world and savouring gossipy speculation about everyone and everything we saw.

As the evening progressed everywhere - on water and land - was becoming busier and busier. We had heard that it was the festival of Il Redentore (something, I think, about redemption - which, I reflected, was one therapy we were not seeking) and that there were to be fireworks at midnight.

From our balcony, the scale of the gathering became dramatically apparent: people were massing in their tens of thousands along the waterfront, and the huge area of the lagoon - as far as the eye could see in every direction - was filling with thousands of craft: great luxury yachts, power boats, launches, rowing boats, gondolas - many decorated

Off for a restful few hours afloat

The New York skyline slips past as the QE2 steams out

with flowers and lanterns - one absurd floating Noddy carboat and an extraordinary pontoon with columns, arches and a cupola picked out with hundreds of coloured light bulbs: on this festive construction a jazz band played as it made its mysterious progress in the dark around the lagoon. Here and there were the flashing blue lights of police launches and everywhere there were lights, music, the noise of exuberant parties, and the sounding of hooters and klaxons.

An area near the mouth of the Grand Canal was clear of boats and there were several dark pontoons in the middle of it: the launch-pad for the fireworks, we presumed.

Around midnight the show began. A hush fell over the City as the first fireworks burst into life. For the best part of an hour there was the grandest, most exuberant, most varied and spectacular display of pyrotechnics the world as probably ever seen: climax after climax tantalised us into thinking it was the finale; time and time again it resumed with more and more extravagant effects - filling the sky with colour and noise till it seemed that more excitement and exhilaration could not possibly be created or enjoyed.

Finally, it was over, and the lagoon and the waterfront erupted in ecstatic shouting and applause; every noise-making instrument known to man was vigorously employed - and every hooter, klaxon and horn was sounded in a deafening, cacophonous tribute of appreciation. It was utterly breathtaking.

It seemed to me a wonderful launch for our trip - a symbolic welcome and send-off which marked my mood and my feeling about what we were doing. Roy was never given

to quite such extravagant notions as I - or, at least, not to
their endless iteration: he watched the show thoughtful and
reflective.

The next day we woke up very uneasy and out of tune
with the world. There was no ill-will between us, but we
were both, separately, edgy and fractious, each overcome by
some inner dislocation, and it would have been very easy to
have had an irrelevant row. Plans for the day had to be
negotiated with a caution and delicacy which were quite
untypical. We agreed to take a vaporetto to the lido and
after two or three hours of walking round the shops and
sitting on the sand, the uneasy mood began to shift,
decisions became simpler and relative harmony slowly
returned. It was much our most difficult and unsatisfactory
day and I am far from clear what lay behind it: it may have
been some perverse or protective reaction to the high
pleasure of the previous day, or to the freedom and intensity
of the whole enterprise. Whatever it was, the mood did not
return.

Venice ended splendidly: the hotel's motor launch - a
grand affair, all polished wood and brass - took us in the
bright morning sun - in our elegant outfits (me in my
Panama and feeling grand) - at first pottering through the
canals and then, in open water, throttles wide, bow high,
stern-flag cracking in the wind, powering ahead as the
ancient City receded - to the unambiguously twentieth
century airport, and the vast transition from medieval
Europe to present-day India.

* * * *

A festive welcome and stylish dining

Two elegant chaps : QE2 studio shot

Of all the places we visited, out of all the memorable things we did and saw, India moved and impressed and unsettled us above all: our brief and superficial acquaintance with that great, mysterious and complex culture fascinated and haunted us; it was the experience we most frequently reverted to in our own conversation and recounted when we met other travellers.

It was our first time in Asia. We had little idea of what to expect, and, in the event, even less idea of how to make sense of the endlessly overwhelming sensations: our affluent Western faculties did not provide easy insight or accurate empathy.

Our few days were spent in the Golden Triangle - Delhi, Agra, Jaipur - with our own car and driver, staying in very good, international hotels.

The sights themselves were, of course, deeply impressive: one cannot but be moved by being in the evocative presence of the Taj Mahal, its tragic and romantic origins, the glory of its construction and the astonishing culture and civilisation out of which it - and so many other grand achievements - flourished. To see it in reality for the first time is, in some strange way, like coming home, experiencing something which has been a vivid image, a presence, a knowledge, a destination for one's entire life.

The glories of the great abandoned city of Fatipur Sikhri and of the Amber Palace on its rocky, mountain ridge; the resonant atmosphere of Raj Ghat where Gandhi was cremated, of Agra Fort and the oppressive, alien pretention of the colonial buildings in Delhi - all remain vivid memories. Our journey on an elephant up the hillside to the Amber Palace filled us with child-like delight - travelling 'like kings for the day' as our driver had promised us (though it has to be said that the Royal Tapestries on which we sat appeared to be more accurately described as threadbare old carpets). We were followed some of the way by a gaunt, bent old man making exquisite sounds with a bow on a single-stringed instrument. We threw him some rupees (worth just pennies) and for the rest of the climb, by turns, he played and expressed his abject gratitude time and time again, much to our discomfort.

Above all, it was the people who transfixed our minds and hearts and left us intrigued and bewildered - and deeply unsettled.

In the cocoon of our very modest, unpredictably air-conditioned car, driving about five hundred miles or so in scorching temperatures, we were assaulted with so much drama and colour that we were left breathless.

First, in Delhi, it was the apparently total, death-defying chaos on the roads: torrents of cars, bicycles, trucks, buses, rickshaws, scooters, jeeps, and pedestrians - many carrying or pulling huge loads - all speeding about in all directions without any evidence of order or priority; we would turn into some side road and be faced with a surging tide of motorised and pedalling humanity bearing down towards us: our driver would simply lean on his horn and put his foot down: this advancing torrent of multitudinous faces and vehicles, somehow, at the very last moment, opened to let us through, swirling together again immediately behind us.

In the early stages of this dramatic initiation into Asian road conditions, we sat gripping our seats, frequently with eyes closed, our hearts pounding every time our driver - or anyone else - sounded a horn or hooter - and that was about every two seconds.

Apart from this overwhelming sense of imminent mortal peril to ourselves and all other road-users, other powerful impressions were also forming: impressions of dilapidation, disorder, poverty and disability. We were quite unprepared for the Third World.

As we drove out of Delhi and eventually into open country - on the trunk roads most traffic going in one direction actually kept mostly to the same side of the road (though junctions, sacred cows and rampant individualists continued to provide frequent heart-stopping excitement) - we saw the naked body of a dead child on the central reservation, the most poignant image of the endless, staggering carnage on the roads which came to haunt and oppress us. On the main trunk road from Jaipur to Delhi there were the remains of major accidents every few miles: head-on collisions between buses and trucks; burnt out vehicles overturned lying in ditches; mangled vehicles in heaps across the road - it was terrifying - and even more so for knowing that every vehicle would have been packed with people inside, with dozens of others perched atop trucks and buses or hanging from the sides. This evidence of slaughter - in the pursuit, we speculated, of fast commerce - made us depressed and cynical.

Everywhere there was evidence of toiling humanity: huge burdens being pushed or carried or dragged, on foot, on bikes, on scooters or carts; women in bright saris with baskets of aggregate on their heads, shovels in their hands, making roads; endless little trading huts and stalls, and everywhere, even in remote country, piles of tyres and wheels and axles and pools of oil and mud.

Disability, deformity and disease were evident everywhere. While the majority of people looked fresh and clean, the men shaved and neat, the women poised and elegant; evidence of confidence and cheerfulness everywhere, the underlying reality of poverty and disadvantage was, to us, powerfully obvious.

All these judgements and observations are seductively easy for an outsider to make: we knew that most of what we saw we could not understand or feel as the people themselves would understand or feel it, and that we would ascribe very different meanings to everything from our alien, Western perspective. Much remained a complete mystery to us, but that did not prevent much moving and unsettling us profoundly. Roy, especially, was depressed by the sense of how cheaply he felt human life seemed to be valued.

In the hotels we could allow ourselves to feel less vulnerable to all the moral and cultural sensitivities of intruding upon the lives of those we could not communicate with or make sense of: here, the roles, at least, were largely unambiguous, though we were very sensitive - as always - about showing respect and courtesy to those who were serving us.

Oddly enough, the spacious bar and one of the restaurants in the Delhi hotel were kitted out in faithful imitation of the Orient Express - diners sitting at the windows of a reconstructed carriage while pre-dinner drinks were taken, as it were, on the station platform. The ambience was subdued and civilised, the young Indian staff all dressed in authentic Orient Express uniforms - the whole show anachoristically surreal. A fluent pianist played Scott Joplin, Gershwin, Novello and Johann Strauss while we drank Indian champagne whimsically branded 'Madame de Pompadour'.

As we found almost everywhere, the staff were gentle, courteous and attentive - at times, perhaps, unnervingly submissive - and often, to my eyes, quite beautiful too. In Agra, in the spectacular clothing of Rajasthan, one felt honoured by the attention of such noble creatures.

In the Orient Express bar, the evening after our frantic introduction to Delhi, we had one of those glorious, intimate, relaxed times - with drinks and nibbles, effortless conversation and an expansive sense of well-being, privilege and wonder.

Roy had a horror of what he always called 'creepie-crawlies' and he had been anxious about the possible invasion of his person by nameless Asian beasties. A notice on the window of the hotel in Jaipur warning of the dangers of flying insects was not reassuring, and it was that evening, when we were having a room service snack, that one of the memorable little comic episodes of the trip occurred.

Roy was putting some kind of red sauce on his food when a real or imagined shadow passed across his vision. He shrieked and flung his hands in the air, simultaneously spraying an arc of sauce across himself and the wall. He leapt up and pranced about the room pursued by the phantom creature before we both dissolved into helpless laughter.

He stripped and went into the shower, and emerged afterwards doing a kind of whimsical, mock-Oriental dance, his brain clearly having been turned by this close encounter with an imagined winged horror.

We later learnt that the mirage was probably caused by a 'floater' in his infected eye: clusters of cells float in the jelly of the eyeball and can look quite grotesque.

* * * *

In Hong Kong Roy's stomach and bowels allowed him little sleep and we called the hotel's doctor, without much hope of his being able to help. He was more interested in the Hickman line than Roy's symptoms and prescribed more tablets which - considering the symptoms - really seemed quite beside the point. They didn't help, if, indeed, Roy even took them (I suspect not).

Hong Kong was enriched for us by spending time with a friend of Roy's (with whom he had worked at London Transport) and her husband. The company and guidance of people who knew the place was a great pleasure. Roy and Lynn went off together a number of times - including an expedition to the famous Pennsylvania Hotel for elegant afternoon tea. We had a lovely afternoon strolling through Stanley Market, visiting a little temple (where we were given great, shiny red apples by a woman in attendance), and sitting lazily by the seafront drinking beer. Most of the time, Roy managed wonderfully during the day, however chaotic the nights. We almost always had two or three hours' sleep in the afternoons.

We went to a tailor and were measured for cotton and silk shirts, travelled on the trams and ferries, and had one or two sumptuous meals then sadly prepared ourselves for the flight across the Pacific.

We had a one-night stopover in San Francisco (our second visit) and I was to dash up the coast to Sonoma Country to visit a potential client for my business - a champagne grower and producer whose marketing team I had previously met in London and Bordeaux. It was a glorious, sparkling Californian day, and I was treated with generous hospitality while my driver and his car baked in the parking lot.

When I returned in the late afternoon, Roy was emerging from a long sleep and we showered and dressed and set off to snatch a ride on a cable-car before wandering along Fisherman's Wharf (where, to our astonishment, there were dozens of vast, basking, barking sea lions) before settling down to a sumptuous meal of seafood and fish.

Roy had discovered a passion for oysters on our previous visit to California. He had had them on the Orient Express and in Venice, but those were as nothing to the glorious dozen served within sight of the Golden Gate that evening. It filled me with happiness to see him able to take such fancy pleasures with such gusto.

* * * *

We arrived at the resort hotel on Montego Bay, Jamaica, late the next evening. Our apartment - with bathroom, small kitchenette and spacious bedroom - was cool and fresh. We opened the shuttered windows and there, ten yards away, beyond a leaning palm tree, the Caribbean Sea was lapping gently on the white sand. Such a simple statement of fact belies the feeling of incredulity and excitement we felt: here, now, this very minute we were, once again, fulfilling the dreams of a lifetime.

We both slept wonderfully that night and woke to the sound of the sea and to arrows of brilliant sunlight coming through the shutters.

Outside was, like so much else we had seen, a picture - in the sense that it was the distillation of all the pictures we had ever seen of tropical beaches and sparkling turquoise seas, but here, now, it was the real thing with us in the midst of it.

After an exotic Caribbean open-air breakfast buffet - with fifty items to choose from - we did very little the next day. Roy could not at first be tempted into the clear, warm water - fearing some malign creature would emerge from beneath his feet and scare him to death - but later went for a paddle, lost his balance and sat down with a splash and a shriek. He sat for some time being rocked by the little waves.

I bought some snacks, we drank a bottle of the champagne I'd been given in California, snoozed, chatted, rigged up the medical gear, and dozed again. We hardly left the apartment. It was lovely.

It was so lovely that we did not want to leave, fearing the Barbados could be only an anti-climax.

Happily it was not. Indeed, our first floor suite was even better, with a deep, furnished balcony overlooking the beach, and all the fixtures and fittings necessary for comfort and indulgence.

There was an excellent restaurant, full of vigorous palms, shrubs and flowers, with its long wall open to the sea; an extensive, airy lounge with cushioned cane furniture where we sat, took delicious afternoon tea (petite sandwiches and freshly baked, moist cakes) or had our pre-dinner drinks.

We took a bus to the capital, Bridgetown - some ten miles away - where we strolled through the market and Roy drank the sweet water of a fresh, green coconut; we took a tour of the north of the island in a taxi driven by Victor, who had been a bus driver for London Transport at Hammersmith garage for twenty-odd years and had returned home - and saw the wild, rocky eastern side of the island with its Atlantic rollers and surfing beaches; and, on the last day, dived in a real submarine which took us within inches of thousands of exotic fish, coral and long-sunken wrecks - more vivid and exciting than any TV documentary.

On our last evening we dined in the restaurant at a table immediately overlooking the beach and the sea. In the evening warmth there was a slight, cooling breeze as the last of the sunset faded. As we ate and talked, there was a glittering display by a shoal of flying fish a hundred yards out to sea - their silvery sides catching the lights from the shore - while nearer in two turtles paddled along and a great manta undulated past.

* * * *

From the moment we landed, New York provided us with problems and disappointments. At JFK immigration it took nearly an hour and a half to get through and Roy was tired and uncomfortable. We were driven through torrential rain to our hotel opposite Madison Square Gardens, where there was no one to help us with the luggage (it was the first and only time abroad we'd had to carry it) and the check-in lines were nearly as long as they'd been at the airport.

Tired, wet and irritated we eventually got to our room which turned out to be a pokey rabbit-hutch in a scruffy and neglected state. The prospect of waiting in lines to negotiate another room was just too much, so we gloomily resigned ourselves to third best and went to bed. (Later I did protest vigorously to the management.)

The next morning, the crisis struck swiftly, and for a few moments we looked into the pit of capitulation and despair.

Roy sat on the edge of the bed, on the verge of tears and said quietly that he simply couldn't keep going any longer: everything was simply too much - too much movement, discomfort, effort; he wanted to be home, in one place, comfortable and undisturbed.

In a split second, everything disintegrated about me: how could we board the QE2 if he was feeling so wretched? What point was there in anything if he was exhausted and unhappy? What was left? My reserves of strength - which had served so wonderfully while they were fed by his drive - seemed to evaporate on the instant: I felt helpless, weak, despairing. I hugged him, sitting beside him, my head on his shoulder and cried too. Persuasion and cajoling were beside the point - even had I felt the energy to try.

Looking squarely in the face of what seemed to be inevitable, responding to his unreserved resignation, I said, if he was sure, that we'd take the next available flight home.

All this took only a matter of minutes, and then something magical happened: out of helpless vulnerability he started to climb back: no, we couldn't do that; after so long and so much we couldn't give up on the last six days, perhaps we could just do something gentle and restful that day. We sat in each other's arms for a time, and I felt my strength surging back as his drive and courage reasserted themselves.

So, we took a yellow cab to the Natural History Museum where we were delighted by the flora and fauna of the world all displayed with colourful imagination. We paused to rest wherever there were seats, giggled at two of the most enormous female bottoms we had ever seen plonked on one of them, and had chips and hamburgers in the café. We emerged into the sunlight to spend the afternoon in Central Park, marvelling at the skaters and bikers and the startling variety of humanity displaying themselves in every possible flamboyant way.

I marvelled at our achievement - especially his: a day that had started in such darkness flourishing into a peaceful and comfortable time. For a few moments that morning some spectre had whispered to us, 'Give up, it's futile', and, hearing and understanding the message clearly, we had been stirred by the challenge - stirred in ways and at levels far beyond reason and thought:

making the choice between life and death while there was still strength to choose. It was the first time, I think, too, that I glimpsed our utter inter-dependence - a mysterious and wonderful process which intertwined our energies and our souls somewhere beyond knowing or control, which made us one while still distinct and separate. There was to be much more to learn of that much later.

* * * *

It was with real excitement that we took our yellow cab to the docks where the QE2 was berthed. The great ship towered above us as we arrived and we felt ourselves instantly in the capable hands of a truly professional, quality operation.

The departure hall was decked with red, white and blue streamers and balloons, and a four-piece band in dinner suits played popular tunes (including 'The Best of Times is Now' from La Cage aux Folles) as we arrived - perfect music for an occasion of such evident, liberated campery.

The cabin was spacious and comfortable - fresh strawberries and chocolates awaiting - two port-holes; TV and video; copious information and sweet messages of welcome.

Everything was, once again, just as it should be - elegant, relaxed, utterly civilised and warmly embracing.

Steaming out of New York in bright afternoon sunshine was thrilling: here we were on the most famous ship in the world, watching the world's most famous skyline slipping past us on a bright, glorious afternoon.

As Manhattan receded astern, contentment settled, and we set about the serious business of exploring the vast acreage of our luxurious home across the Atlantic.

* * * *

There are about ten or a dozen degrees of first-class travel on the QE2 and we were in something like category five - pretty impressive, we felt, but a long way from the £10,000 penthouse suites at the top of the list (1991 prices). £10,000 seemed a lot for five nights, even with the provision of your own permanent staff! (One evening we met the occupants of one of the penthouse suites in one of the dozens of lifts - who were so old and frail they couldn't find their way back and were as vulnerable and helpless as lost children.)

We were allocated to the category two restaurant (the Colombia) which offered the most spectacular food and service we had experienced anywhere ever: menus of such comprehensiveness, dishes of such seductive deliciousness that it was depressing to have to choose only one for each of the endless courses. On our table for six, there was just one American couple with whom we had amiable chat. Our assigned waiters were splendid - kind, attentive and with that subdued campness which can make service such fun.

It would easily have been possible to do nothing but eat for the duration of the entire voyage: in the restaurant, multi-course feasts were provided for breakfast, lunch and dinner; there was a massive lunchtime buffet elsewhere; if you risked sitting down anywhere between three and five o'clock you'd find giant afternoon tea being piled in front of you; and there was a full-scale midnight buffet for those who were still feeling peckish before retiring. This last, in spite of our ambition to sample it, we never finally felt the inclination - or the hunger - to visit or enjoy.

'Informal dress' for dinner required lounge suits, while on formal nights dinner jackets were *de rigueur.* Dressing up was part of the fun, and though I never thought of myself as handsome (in contrast to Roy who was), I thought we made a pretty impressive couple and I felt proud as we walked the ship.

We were struck by the (I suppose obvious) fact that the QE2 is utterly untainted by utilitarian purposes: no one is going to take that mode of transport to get quickly between New York and Southampton, and so it follows that everyone is aboard for no purpose other than self-indulgence (many, we discovered, had sailed on her many times before and there was a Captain's cocktail party for old hands): such an elaborate operation, such resources, such skill, such a weight of strawberries, such a volume of champagne, such human effort for sheer pleasure! We were, indeed, among the privileged.

Roy was much less troubled by sickness and diarrhoea than he had been; his body and spirit were comforted by the motion of the ship and the simple, effortless, cocooned existence. As the days passed, we thought sadly of our approach to Southampton and the grey skies of Britain and the cool hand of reality. Yet, it must also be recorded, we felt a profound sense of achievement and fulfilment, of consummation, even satiation, and did not hanker for more: we had attempted what could have seemed impossible and we had, in so many ways, triumphed against the odds. There was little, if anything, left on our agenda of dreams.

We knew we were home when we were greeted at Waterloo with unapologetic unhelpfulness, hopeless disorganisation and were left to struggle to the taxi rank with our luggage without any risk of assistance.

The DIARY

Part III

September 1991 - February 1992

It's now midnight on Saturday 24 August, just one week after our return - and what one hell of a week this has been! Roy's diarrhoea and stomach problems have deteriorated rapidly, and he had very little inclination to eat. On the Sunday, the day after our return, we'd had a lovely day with Eric and Audrey, and Roy had had a little bit of the picnic which they had so thoughtfully brought for us. He seemed in quite good form though tired, and had a sleep in the afternoon. Most of Monday he spent in bed and made an appointment to see his consultant at the clinic the following day. He was in reasonable spirits and in the afternoon went out and posted the sick note and a letter of explanation to his employers.

He went to the appointment on Tuesday and Jo said that he should be admitted to hospital, particularly for treatment to his eye, but also to give attention to the other problems. The first I knew was when he phoned me at work around 5 o'clock and said that he was in hospital. My first sensation was one of considerable relief that he was now going to be properly looked after and with some hope that the problems would be sorted out quickly. My selfish anxiety about his being in hospital again was that my days would once more take on the endless and restless pattern, out to work early in the morning and back to home late at night, having gone straight from work to the hospital. It's terribly exhausting and makes managing the house, keeping my brain in order and resting almost impossible. I have to be thankful that the hospital is relatively accessible.

Now, the alarming fact is that since being in hospital he seems to have gone downhill. Last night, Friday, I came home quite late, very depressed, fearing that he really did not have much longer to live. Early yesterday he had been in a very bad way after the first dose of Foscarnet and he refused further doses. He was clearly in very low spirits and very under the weather though he did revive a little towards the end of the day. He's been weighed and is now around eleven and a half stone - nearly two stone less than a few weeks ago. He has eaten virtually nothing, though on Wednesday he did ask me to get him a couple of Kentucky Fried Chicken drumsticks and sent me out for a further two which he ate cold the following day. A few mouthfuls of milk and milky nutrient foods are all he's had, and he appears to be passing out more liquid than he's taking in.

Today, Saturday, I was with him for about eight hours from mid-afternoon and he was quite lively, especially when Keith turned up, but became tired and depressed as the day went on. He is still having to go to the loo very frequently and after taking his Pentamadine today was sick, nullifying the effects of the porridge he had at breakfast and the tablets he would have taken during the day. I thought as I saw him lying in bed that he was looking exceptionally thin and frail and helpless.

Today we tackled the staff about the diarrhoea which they had been allowing to continue largely in order to have enough samples for testing. Today we said really that it was time that they did try to do something to stop the symptoms and to see if it was not possible to get some sort of nourishment into him. The upshot of this was a decision to give him diamorphine in tiny doses from a battery-driven syringe-driver over 24 hours (one of the potent effects of morphine is to bind the bowels). I just hope he also has some of the agreeable side-effects that morphine might be expected to give him!

He's currently having a treatment dose of Ganciclovir (380 mgs twice a day) and they are leaving him on a saline or potassium drip overnight (I think it's a litre each time) in order to prevent dehydration - his skin is beginning to flake, and his weight loss is continuing.

I had a chat with Jane (ward Sister) on Thursday asking her what she thought the problem was and what could be done. She was saying that they really didn't know and only the return of the samples would indicate whether or not he had CMV infection in his gut as well as his eye, which would give us some indication as to whether or not he was in the last steep decline of the syndrome, or just under a temporary attack from some bug. On Thursday, certainly, he was feeling so awful that he said that he didn't want to go on if he was going to feel like that. He said today that for the first time he had become genuinely worried about the future, obviously feeling worse and less hopeful than he has done at any time so far. There's little to do at such times except accept and support and to see if the drugs cannot be altered to reduce discomfort.

We've got tickets for the performance by the New York City Gay Men's Choir tomorrow night, Sunday, and Nurse John, when he heard about that today, said that Roy really ought to go and that he would ring up the Royalty Theatre and ask them to make sure there was a disabled seat available for him near an exit so that he could get out quickly if necessary. Roy had already seemed keen to go to the performance, and this helpful and reassuring suggestion brightened him up. We were both very impressed and grateful - John and other members of staff on the ward do seem to be endlessly resourceful and thoughtful. We will just have to hope that the effects of the diamorphine do not sedate him too much and that he actually has the strength to get from the bed to the front of the hospital to pick up a cab. When he tried to walk out with me on Thursday afternoon he couldn't get beyond the entrance, feeling weak and faint.

It feels as though we're in the midst of a crisis and it will be some days before we know whether it is temporary or whether it is the beginning of the end.

Thank god we went round the world when we did - had we left it even a week or two it might have been impossible. And it's now clear that his sheer determination to see it through postponed this latest and serious deterioration.

What I don't quite know, and it concerns me, is how I am going to survive if he is going to become progressively ill. The business requires a tremendous amount of attention and effort at the moment, and I have to be able to clear my mind and to have resources, energy and imagination to drive us forward into a successful and prosperous 1991/92. If all my spare time is to be absorbed by going to the hospital - which obviously I want to do - spending as much time with him as I can and looking after him - it has such a draining effect on my emotions and my energy that I don't know if I shall be able to cope. Even although this is a bank holiday, I am uncertain that I will be able to cut the wildly overgrown hedge and lawn and attend to the ordinary things which are necessary to keep the house and garden in order.

I woke this morning feeling very depressed and lost, but pulled round a bit after talking to friends on the phone. While having him at home would obviously be a much greater pleasure, and would reduce the strain to some extent, it worries me to think of him being here on his own during the day and that in itself is a distracting anxiety. I am very concerned, however, at the way in which his recent and rather more dramatic decline seems to have taken place since he went into hospital - I'm sure lying in bed all day, while it is obviously very therapeutic in some ways, actually undermines the body's capacity to cope with things, reduces muscular strength, the effectiveness of blood circulation and everything else and compounds an already considerable weakness. I also have to remember that if, as seems certainly to be the case, Roy's psychology has some direct effects on illness, there's probably a tendency for him, as it were, to allow illness to get the upper hand in hospital - where it can rapidly be attended to. I don't know what the alternative is, nor what we can do to counteract the effects.

While still very weak, Roy was more cheerful on the day of the concert and was determined to go. Anxiously and slowly we made our way on foot to the theatre - he insisted on walking the mile or so - where he slept intermittently. The programme did not seem as exciting to us as the previous NYGMC concert we'd been to, though it may have had more to do with our inner life than the objective facts of the performance. But we made it - once again Roy defying frailty!

* * * *

It's Thursday evening, 29 August. We learnt yesterday that the infection causing the diarrhoea and vomiting is something called Cryptosporidium*. Sister Jane spent her usual kindly ten or fifteen minutes with me today and told me that it's an infection which is untreatable and all they can hope to do is deal with the symptoms (it's one of those bugs resident in everyone which is more or less harmless in a healthy system). With the frankness that she knows I want, she said that this did indicate that we were into a further stage of the syndrome and that the time left to Roy was shortening. The prediction was for a few weeks at best. Today's good news was that it seems that his eye has not deteriorated further which means that the Ganciclovir and tackle we carried all round the world may have done some good. It also means that he will not have to have any more

Foscarnet which has caused him so much distress over the last few days.

It's been an awful, harassing day for him, though: at 9 o'clock this morning he had a barium meal (which he said wasn't too bad) and was X-rayed and then, having got an ambulance to his eye appointment in the afternoon was kept waiting for the best part of two hours, hanging around, when Jane had organised that he should be seen quickly. When I arrived about 5.30 he was weary and fed up and fell asleep within minutes. After three quarters of an hour or so, however, he had come round and chatted with Nicky and me though he very soon became dopey again. After Nicky had left we both slept together, he leaning against me in my arms on the bed.

While I am impressed with the efforts of the staff to make life for Roy more comfortable, treating the symptoms in the hope that he may be able to eat something and benefit from nourishment - although there is some doubt that his stomach will now ever perform properly at all - there is something grim about the succession of chemicals which they are putting into him, some of which are to counteract the bad side-effects of other ones, several of which are experimental, some of which are certainly toxic and awful, but I don't know what alternative there is. They are scouring the pharmacological armoury thoroughly - but I think it's a pretty hit and miss affair.

While we have faced the whole issue of his death quite squarely from the beginning, it is still not a graspable reality, and I cannot reconcile myself to the possibility that he may never be for any significant length of time the old Roy and indeed may be able to spend only very short periods at home ever again. I cannot imagine life without him. All this has a kind of illusory quality - it's impossible to reconcile the reality of death with his continuing living body even though it is suffering and weak.

Friends have, as in the past, been wonderful - Nicky has been going in each day, an especial comfort to me as there was a risk on Wednesday that I wouldn't get to see him in the evening at all; Terry has been wonderfully supportive and thoughtful, bringing endless bunches of fragrant Casablanca lilies which Roy and I love - he brought me home from the hospital last evening and we sat and had a very brief nightcap and a chat; Peter and Geraldine to whom I spoke for the first time tonight since we returned were touchingly concerned and made the wonderfully practical and helpful offer of doing the shopping for me at the weekend when they went to Sainsbury's and delivering it here. (The great struggle at the moment is simply keeping the practical arrangements of life going and giving myself the odd few minutes each day simply to look at the post, to sit down, to read the paper, to think about what needs to be done to keep the house in order); Cathy has been in to see him; Sue went in earlier in the week and I think gave him a great boost - she seems so ebullient and strong and purposeful now - there was a phone call later in the evening from her, and she struck me as enormously strong and determined, not only for herself but for Roy too. Eric and Audrey and Mary on the phone have been immensely warm, supportive and generous, offering, like so many, to do anything they can to help.

I spoke to Vera tonight and presented the latest news fairly squarely and coolly, without being over gloomy or providing false hopes. She is hoping to come down with Amanda on Monday and stay overnight to see Roy on two days. I was initially rather taken aback by the proposal to stay overnight but made it clear that that was fine (others have rights, too!)

I haven't cried a lot, but I get very near to it as I sit by Roy's bed holding his hand, as he sleeps, looking so helpless and with so little to look forward to. He is still there, he is still holding on to himself, his courage, his spirit, his cheerfulness, his thoughtfulness. I hope he does not lose those great qualities for his own sake and ours.

* * * *

It's the afternoon of Sunday 1st September and Roy has been home now for about 24 hours. He arrived Saturday midday looking very pale and frail, carrying his new bright yellow sharps box. Both of us felt that being in hospital was not doing him good - certainly psychologically. The medical team had no objection to his returning home for the weekend (indeed were keen that he should), though the drugs regime was going to be much more complicated and demanding than before. We sat in the garden for a while, then he had to dash to the loo and didn't make it in time. He was annoyed and upset by the accident. I simply set about cleaning up and helping him out of his clothes. Strange how all one's squeamishness absolutely disappears in such circumstances - the main problem was not being properly equipped with adequate cloths, mops and other equipment.

After a short while he decided to have a shower and I helped him with that and he then chose the brilliant, extravagant, Mary Quant shorts and T-shirt I brought him from Heathrow some months ago. I was much moved that while he was feeling so wretched he was dressing so splendidly. He looked lovely, but the contrast between his weak, pale body and the joyful tropical clothes was hard to endure. (On another occasion when he was looking and feeling miserable he chose the Walk for Life T-shirt (an AIDS charity item) which left me pregnant with tears.)

He had another very close shave a short while later, but managed to save his clothes. I mopped up the loo.

After a while he came in to rest in the front room and snoozed on and off for the next few hours.

Later on in the evening Peter and Geraldine arrived with the great Sainsbury's shop that they had done for us, and we sat around chatting about this and that, the holiday and other things, a conversation to which Roy contributed a little but drifted away every so often.

When Peter and Geraldine arrived, Anne Louise, the community care team registrar also came, renewing the syringe pump and giving him an injection of the trial drug through the Hickman line.

After Peter and Geraldine had gone we sat around in the front room for a time, I cooked myself some supper, we watched a bit of television, though Roy dozed through most of it. It took us a long time to get moving to go to bed and once there we were both very restless and I went off to the spare bed after a couple of hours.

During the night I heard Roy up several times being sick and in the morning it was clear he had slept very little and had had a miserable night.

Anne Louise came again around 10 o'clock and gave him some Hyoscine* which for the rest of the day has made Roy almost comatose, muttering now and then, I suspect hallucinating a little, occasionally shocked when he opens his eyes and finds me sitting next to him. I have to remember that the current state is probably the effect of the drugs, but it is enormously distressing - he's almost incoherent, has a very shaky voice, his coordination is doubtful and all I can hope is that somewhere inside him he is pleased to be home. I really don't know what to do and am feeling at a very loose end, comforting myself with talking to the tape recorder and busying myself with washing and other domestic chores.

After talking to an old friend from the north on Thursday or Friday, and discovering that he had tried to take his life a couple of weeks ago, and that he was obviously in a very bad way, I suggested that he came and stay, something that he had said he had wanted as he was looking for 'a sanctuary'.

He is coming about 6 o'clock tonight, more or less the time when Roy will be going back to hospital. I have no idea if this is a good idea, whether it is going to be a comfort or a burden, but I think the prospect of somebody being around during this time will actually be quite a help although I doubt if our friend will be his usual cheerful self. Amanda and Vera are coming to stay tomorrow for Monday night as well but I am afraid most of the niceties of hospitality may well go by the board on this occasion, though they must be made welcome.

All this stress is not helped by the fact that I am very worried about the business at the moment. July was a bad month with a loss, August I think will be not much better and we really will have to start thinking about major cutbacks, possibly even losses of jobs. I just hope that some decent piece of work comes through very rapidly, or that we manage to generate a substantial amount of income quickly. At the moment I don't feel that anyone is being particularly inventive or resourceful in our sales effort, and I am sure I do not have the energy and imagination and get up and go that is necessary to keep things moving. We have certainly got to act very soon if we are to prevent a serious situation developing.

The business, EQUUS, was just over one year old. There were six staff, a first-year turnover of about £400,000, and shareholders who had put in over £200,000 to get the business going. Even after one year there were only two of us who were significant earners. The pressure to deliver results was huge. Around half of our turnover came from one client (our major shareholder) but that was far from enough to pay the wages and bills on its own. The Company was founded on my reputation and it was I who had to deliver. Apart from the exceptional step of having a whole month off for the world trip, I don't believe any one of my clients (among those I hadn't told) knew there was anything amiss. The business - marketing and training consultancy - involved the delivery of training sessions; the planning and implementing of marketing campaigns; the research, writing and production of a variety of publications. People paid us for our energy and creativity, so we couldn't afford to be performing at less than 100%.

Though a major leitmotif of my professional life and training message was 'The show must go on' whatever might be happening backstage, there's certainly a level at which everything does get a bit mixed up: when, for example, endings in one aspect of life prompt pessimistic and destructive feelings and reactions in a quite different aspect. It was quite a complicated act of will to express and enact a bright and expanding future for the business while, at home, almost every emotional resource was devoted to adjusting to progressive decline and ultimate death.

* * * *

It's the evening of Sunday 8 September and it's now about two hours since Peter and Geraldine drove Roy back to the hospital.

Having just listened to the last couple of sentences of the previous entry, I need to add something of a corrective: it turns out that sales in August were rather better than I had feared, though still far from adequate, and what I think was probably a rather gloomy feeling at the time of the last writing has moved on a little to greater optimism and hope. It's nevertheless the case that we still have an enormous amount to achieve in terms of sales and have got to improve our performance and profitability dramatically.

For me the last week has been much better than previously: I think I have now fully recovered from the anti-climax of returning to the UK after our trip; I have begun to come to terms with the inescapable realities of Roy's health; have begun to get back into my stride at work and have already taken a number of initiatives and had some excellent ideas.

For most of the week back in hospital Roy has been very dopey and hallucinating a good deal from the exotic cocktail of drugs they're giving him. On one occasion when I was sitting by his bed holding his hand, he was tugging violently at it; when he opened his eyes said that he had been trying to draw some curtains and thought my hand was one of them; on another occasion, which he has repeated to a number of people with amusement, Nicky and I were sitting with him when he was drinking a glass of milk and he found himself putting two fingers in the glass, evidently having thought that it was a jar of pickled onions and trying to get an onion out. The week's been full of peculiarities of that kind, including his talking to people who weren't there, thinking people who were there were actually someone else and so on. It's been quite distressing from the point of view of having very little opportunity of coherent communication, though he has been very relaxed and available during his lucid moments - which can end at a second's notice with his eyes rolling upwards and his eyelids closing. It's been odd from the point of view that in some senses he really hasn't been there and much of the time I've spent with him has been in silence, either just holding his hand or on one very agreeable occasion, dozing on the bed with him, his head on my shoulder. Denise, one of the nurses, told us that she came in for some reason or other, while we were asleep but didn't like to disturb us because, 'We looked like two cherubs!'

He came home yesterday, Saturday, and sat in the front room most of the afternoon and evening, sleeping most of the time, drinking a good deal, eating a little raspberry jelly and ice cream, which he managed to keep down for some time, then went to bed around half past nine or so and seemed to have a quite peaceful night with only a couple of interruptions to go to the loo.

Today, Sunday, seems to have been a very peaceful and refreshing day for him which he spent in bed, sleeping most of the while, coming round every so often to have a drink, to talk to me, to take or make phone calls, but all in a very relaxed way. He himself said that it had been very refreshing to be away from the interruptions and disturbance of the ward - another indication of the perhaps negative effects which being in hospital can have, along with the physical atrophy which sets in through lack of exercise.

At this moment I really don't know how ill he is. I found myself saying in my head on one or two occasions as I sat with him, 'he's dying', and yet I have really no idea. I don't know how a body can continue to survive without eating for so very long and the staff at the hospital seem very reluctant to give him anything substantial which would really sustain him. He is now on intravenous fluids virtually twenty-four hours a day and in addition to the ordinary saline, they are giving him a potassium and saline drip, alternating with a saline, potassium and glucose drip. On Friday they gave him three units of 400 millilitres of blood as his haemoglobin had dropped. That should provide some degree of nourishment and refreshment for the system.

This evening he actually did seem much more chirpy, though he is still vomiting up even the glasses of water he's drinking while the diarrhoea seems to have been controlled to some extent - though there are still urgent and quite frequent calls.

Our friends continue to be wonderful:, phoning up, calling, visiting, offering practical help. Peter and Geraldine again suggested that they might come and take Roy back to the hospital. Originally I had intended to go back with him, but took the opportunity of a few hours tonight to get myself together. There's the phone again.

* * * *

It's the evening of Sunday 15 September and Roy has just returned to hospital and phoned up to say that he was back. We've been using his Taxicard regularly with one company who seem to be enormously efficient - arrive on time, pleasant drivers, modern, smart vehicles - altogether very well organised. With the £7.75 contribution made by the Taxicard the journey usually costs about £6.50 or so each way.

(We have had some awful journeys, though: having to stop the taxi every few minutes for Roy to throw the door open and be sick in the gutter. He, especially, hates anything which is messy or public. I find it quite hard too.)

Last week saw Roy's condition improving relatively dramatically: after having the blood the Friday before last weekend, the restful weekend at home, and then being on virtually 24 hour tpn drip (total parenteral nutrition) and the various kinds of adjustments they are making to the drug regime. By Wednesday, Thursday, Friday he was really almost back to his normal self, bright, alert, sleeping very little during the day with energy back in his voice and eyes.

This weekend at home, he has been very tired and washed out, though yesterday lunchtime he had some soup and cheese and wasn't sick until late in the evening when he said he fancied pancakes with lemon and sugar but was sick after two or three mouthfuls of the first one. He slept well and this morning fancied a soft boiled egg and 'dippy' soldiers which he ate and enjoyed. (I'm so happy that he actually wants things and I can get them for him.)

We went through the quite elaborate drug regime this morning - one intravenous direct into the Hickman line; one which had to be made up with a bag of saline and taken over an hour or so; followed by a third and a flush of Heplok.

Because he's been fairly weary, we haven't had much conversation, though we slept together on the bed yesterday and snoozed this afternoon on the sofa.

All week he'd been saying that he fancied a proper roast Sunday lunch, and had asked me to get some beef or lamb. I got a leg of lamb and did that today with Yorkshire pudding and potatoes and whatnot but come the time he had no stomach for it, and I stuffed myself quietly in the kitchen with a glass of wine. He had a morsel or two of lamb later. I actually found myself not caring in the least about the effort involved in any of these things - the pancakes last night or the lamb today - my overriding interest is in providing him with anything that he feels he has the slightest chance of eating.

This evening as he sat snoozing on the sofa, he looked so pale and fragile - his eyes really are sunken now, and his face really looks gaunt - I thought again with horror that he would look like that when he was dead. It's so difficult to know what the prospects are, whether his body will ever start functioning properly on its own again or whether he'll be totally dependent on the food and drugs which are being pumped into him in such huge quantities. There was the realisation this weekend that without the virtually 100% support of intravenous feeding and total care he could probably not carry on at all.

We've talked about the weekends, and are hoping that he'll manage to get home for as many as possible and we've talked too of his coming home for good - though I have no idea whether that is a reasonable possibility; whether he will be able to manage on his own while I'm out at work.

We had another member of the community care team come round last night, in fact twice because the ward had not sent all the drugs that were necessary. She was absolutely splendid, committed, interested, concerned to make sure that she and the team provided everything that Roy wanted for his comfort and to fulfil the things he wanted to achieve. Really very impressive, and another element of the service we've been given which has greatly impressed us and for which we are very grateful.

I hover between depression and anxiety about him and from time to time the guilty feeling that I wish it was all over. But he is still well enough to take some pleasure in coming home and to look forward to events in the future. While there's hope of him having some good days we must carry on with confidence and optimism though I feel his resources are so weak I can't really imagine what's going to happen.

I've sat down with a glass of whisky tonight but I'm surprised and pleased how little I've taken to drink to get through.

I still really do not know what it is like for him - he still seems to have such spirit on his good days and there seems to be no sign of despair, anger, frustration and no expression of suffering. He is remarkable.

* * * *

Soon after that we negotiated his coming home for slightly longer and soon mastered the drugs regime and the new techniques required.

In fact, it was all coming together rather easily, and I popped home at lunchtimes to see to the midday routines.

* * * *

During the last couple of weeks back in hospital Roy has been in a much better state with the nausea and diarrhoea much more satisfactorily controlled, though he has been very dopey and slept a large percentage of each day. He's had quite a few visitors, including Eric who popped in on a London day as did Jeremy. Both weeks I have had to spend two days in Newcastle, and Nicky has visited in my absence.

Today, Ann phoned up asking if Vera could come down next weekend with Lily and Cyril. Both Roy and I, quite independently, came to the conclusion that we wanted our weekends left quiet and peaceful and while he phoned Ann and told her this, I wrote to Lily and Cyril on Vera's behalf telling them about Roy's illness and also to Vera, enclosing a copy of the letter, indicating our thoughts about weekend visits. Roy said, 'We are not pawns in a game,' and we decided that we had to stay in control and not simply give way to every wish expressed from Yorkshire - or anywhere else for that matter. He remains so quietly strong!

We seem to be making some progress with sorting out his employment issues and have now written to his manager explaining the situation, without being explicit, and are awaiting a response from him in relation to the retirement pension, lump sum or whatever arrangements they are willing to make.

We have applied for mobility and attendance allowances, and those look as though they are going through with the necessity of having an examination by a doctor for the mobility allowance once Roy is at home.

At present we are hoping that he may be home next weekend and then permanently as things this weekend really have worked very well, smoothly and simply and Roy has clearly had great pleasure in being here.

Palliative medicine is doing its work, though at the moment it's at the cost of Roy's lucidity and alertness, though he has many good periods during the day though prone to falling asleep quite unexpectedly. We seem, strangely and inexplicably, to have passed all the main pain and grief barriers, simply taking things as they come day by day, and enjoying what simple pleasures we can - sitting quietly holding hands on the sofa or snoozing in front of some unstimulating television programme.

For me, the world is shrinking to home with him, his hospital bed, and, of course, business. Beyond that very little has any strong or compelling reality in spite of being in the midst of a great, throbbing capital city.

* * * *

It's midnight on Sunday 6 October. Roy came home on Thursday evening permanently, a prospect which, I think, had lightened both our moods during the preceding days. I felt a huge sense of relief that we were going to return to as near normal as we could and that the physical burden of hospital visiting would be stopped.

It's been great having him around, comforting, peaceful, a return to some sort of companionship, conversation and a more natural rhythm of communication.

But he is not happy. Out of hospital, and with the distractions of hospital routine out of the way, he is painfully aware of his incapacity, his weakness, the fact that he never feels in good form even after a sound night's sleep.

Today he said he really did not want to go on feeling as he does now and asked if I had had any conversations with the doctors about how long he had left.

He can do none of the things that used to give us so much pleasure - eating a meal with a bottle of wine here or out in town, having a night out at the theatre, even (as he said) having a pint of beer in a pub. At present he is not strong enough to go out of the house to the shops or for a walk on the common; he really hardly has the energy to stay awake in front of a television programme - there's nothing to look forward to, nothing that is full of pleasure.

We agreed that I would phone the on-call community care team member and raise the question of quality of life: they could then consider the option of starting him on steroids* as they had suggested. He was in no doubt that quality was what mattered and he had no interest in lingering on helpless and weak.

He has been depressed, too, by the apparent complications and difficulties of the medical regime, anxious about how he is to cope when I am not here, even the quite simple routines which we managed to go through without thinking on the world trip are now a source of anxiety and take him a great length of time. His deteriorating sight is such that he has difficulty in placing a needle accurately in an ampoule or in the line, and from time to time he does not have the strength to undo the bung or disconnect the drips. (I've had difficulty with some of them.) Some of the anxieties seemed to lift when I said that the great majority of the routines I could do and on occasions when I was going to be away we could make sure that a nurse or one of the community care team came in to help. But those are trivial issues beside the one big one.

So death has been on both our minds today, and as I sit here while he sleeps upstairs I think of it too and wonder how I shall cope. I find myself preparing for it in a way which accepts its inevitability yet I am horrified by the risk of resignation to it. It seems tragic that so much human effort, so much medical resource can do so little to affect or reverse the irresistible progress of disease. Yet, I suppose, what we have now, a degree of stability and comfort, is so much better than a month ago with the constant state of distress and emergency. Yet it's no life, and though there's the tiny chance of a period of remission, the present quality is probably of little value to him, though his continuing existence matters so much to me.

He has eaten a little this weekend - we had soft poached eggs on toast for lunch, and as far as I'm aware he has not been sick, which is great!

While this private tragedy is overwhelming our lives, while we plan to get as simply and comfortably through each day as we can, for me it has heightened an awareness of the millions of tragedies of a similar kind which are happening all the time: those many millions for whom famine and disease are inevitable facts of life with no resources, no comfort, no medicine even to alleviate pain. We are just two people.

We've had the good fortune to have around us the most extraordinary team of nurses and doctors and even today, talking to Anne Louise on the phone there is a degree of commitment, concern and energy which is really remarkable - a commitment to making sure that such time as Roy has left should be as satisfactory as possible in his terms. That's all been remarkable, because in the midst of this, officiousness or indifference would have made it all unbearable.

* * * *

Saturday 2nd November: I think it must be about a month since I have put anything on paper but memories of that period are so overwhelmed by the events of the last couple of days that it is almost a blank to me.

On Friday 25 October a nurse from the ward phoned us to let us know that Keith had died in St Mary's the previous night. (Keith was the other member of the 'Ganciclovir Gang' who used to sit with Roy on the ward talking and giggling as they took their chemo-therapy.) I went back in and told Roy and cried helplessly - I think as much for us as for Keith and Bill, simply overcome by the unstoppable progress of the disease and its shocking, inevitable end.

It was not, I think, until a week later when Bill phoned Roy at home to tell him about the funeral taking place the following day that Roy gave vent to his feelings of sadness and loss. He phoned me at work in tears after talking to Bill who had said affectionate things about Roy's friendship with Keith. I was all for coming home to be with him but he said that was not necessary (he simply wanted to talk with me; he wanted me to get on with my work); though I so much wanted to be with him. I was shaken by the reality of Keith's funeral and by Roy's untypically overt distress and tears.

The next day we arranged a cab to collect Roy from home and to pick me up from work to go on to the

Lighthouse where the service was being held. It was an immensely tearful occasion with many of us crying unashamedly through the service, throats and hearts aching. To be with Roy at such an occasion, frail, ill as he was, struck deep.

The priest was a dead loss, mournful, unemotional, monotonous and I felt the conventional Christian things he had to say were empty, insulting rubbish, which he did not deliver as if even he believed. They did not speak to us, our condition, our beliefs; he did not comfort us, indeed he offended me with his confidence that for Keith the best things were yet to come - an afterlife of rich opportunities and all that. Weren't we searching our souls for ways of making *this* life worthwhile? Weren't we fighting with every resource we had to snatch happiness and pleasure out of darkness and pessimism *now*?

It was what Keith had wanted, but for me it was hollow and unsatisfying, and for Roy, too, I think. Oh for a ceremony to touch the mountainous grief there was in that room - for Keith, for his lover, for the family, for his friends, and for the gay men and their sick and dying friends! Tragic, useless, hurtful, trivial.

Today, Saturday, has been a horrific day. Roy's syringe driver failed to function properly during the night and he's had a day of hideous diarrhoea and emergencies.

We talked early in the morning about his funeral, and made notes of some of the music that he wanted. He said that he wished it had been he who had died and not Keith. He is feeling agitated and unwell, probably, we later realise, the result of withdrawal from the diamorphine which had not been going through the syringe. But that, with the emotional trauma of Keith's death and the funeral, along with the suddenly assertive symptoms today, certainly made him feel that he did not want to go on. He wondered whether we could make the trip to Paris that we'd planned, and suggested cancelling it or selling the tickets. I resisted this and said we should wait and see and that we would get through this bad patch.

It became evident during the day that the malfunction of the syringe driver was probably in the line so we could not put it right. We called the community care team and Vicky came out in the evening to change the line. She, like the rest of the team, was quite splendid, sensitive, thoughtful, attentive and after changing the line gave Roy a strong injection of morphine and an anti-sickness drug which after an hour or so sent him into a deep sleep.

She then spent about an hour and a half with me, wonderfully sensing that I desperately needed to talk today and we went through all the tough stuff.

Roy was not going to die suddenly, she reassured me, and he would probably not die while I was away. We talked a lot about 'moving the goalposts' (her phrase) looking to much shorter term goals, shorter even than the three weeks to our proposed Paris trip. We talked of the tension I feel between my wish to be with Roy most of the time and the requirement, understood by both of us, that I should be at work and attending to the business. She offered the service of their team of volunteers to stay overnight with Roy when I was away if that comforted me, suggesting that whether or not Roy felt it was necessary it may be something he should agree to for my sake. She said that should there be any kind of emergency when I was away from London they would let me know and there would be time for me to get back. Though she comforted me with the observation based on the team's experience that Roy would not die when I was away, she said that people do tend to die when they want to. They, as the team, were also committed to letting people die where they wanted to. I told her that Roy and I were in no doubt that that was to be at home.

We talked a lot about quality of life: Roy clearly feels that the present quality is not sufficient and at the current level he'd rather not go on. Vicky and I agreed that resolving that was a joint task: they should try and lift the physical quality of his life a little while I should attend to providing more short term goals and stimulus to make the days immediately ahead more attractive.

He's had such an awful day today - feeling grotty, erupting bowels, three lots of washing. For my needs, I want him to live; but for his, I know that the life he has is not right for him, does not allow him to be himself, does not satisfy him and the prospects of serious improvement are tiny. I have to learn to let go. While he must know that for my happiness his life remains so precious, I have to recognise too that for him, suffering as he is, that may not be enough. Is certainly not enough.

Jackie came today and took the remaining tropical fish from Roy's tank which is now dark and empty. Roy came down for a few moments while she was here but looked weak and distressed and went almost straight back to bed.

* * * *

25th January: It's now a considerable time since I have committed any thoughts to paper. This is a reflection of the two or three months of pressure at work, unremitting activity and anxiety at home and the passing of such hours or days where there have been periods of freedom, largely sleeping or vacantly watching the TV or video.

Following the appalling crisis of November things for Roy did begin to settle down and with the introduction of steroids the symptoms, particularly of vomiting, were almost completely controlled. They did have the disturbing effect, however, of giving his face a swollen, bloated look.

Up to Christmas, there was a period of really extraordinary stability though I think it was evident that he was becoming more and more radically weary and spending more and more time in bed, usually remaining asleep until midday or later, getting up for a couple of hours, snoozing, perhaps on the sofa, and then being at least partly awake during the evenings when I was at home.

The decision to take the steroids was a significant one, and it was one which was precipitated by Roy's clear choice to have what quality he could during the time remaining. This was something we had talked about with the medical team at the Middlesex and the community care team many months before when we were contemplating leaving hospital and managing the illness at home. The medical team had made it clear to us in the early autumn that we should not expect a very great length of time, and in November in the gentlest, most tentative way, it was indicated again that we should not be deceived by the apparent improvement and stability, and should certainly prepare ourselves for, perhaps, a matter of mere weeks, probably four or five at best.

I can't remember if that precise period was discussed with Roy, but he and I certainly had conversations in which we acknowledged the likely shortness of time, and we prepared ourselves in several ways.

We spent some time with Terry, talking about the funeral arrangements, and the music Roy would like to have. He had some time alone with Terry, and then I joined them and we talked over all the details. We were conscious of the uncanny nature of our conversation, but carried it through with calm, if emotional care and then went on to talk of other things.

Roy was keen also that he should see his mum and she came down with the family. At the time of their visit the drug routines were particularly complex and time-consuming: there was hardly an hour of the day when there weren't tablets to take, drips to be attached or removed, injections into the Hickman line, filling or adjusting the syringe driver. During the time I wasn't cooking or administering drugs, I was in the 'pharmacy' upstairs preparing equipment or mixing the complex cocktails. His mum was shocked at the state of his health and realised that his physical care was beyond her, however much she might long to have him 'home'.

Roy and I had talked about the business of death and I had said how anxious I was that he might die when I was away and that I hoped he would hold on. The nurses on the ward, like Vicky, had said that most people are able to choose the time and place of their death, and that given the will they will die when and where they want. Roy said that for him it would be on the sofa with his head in my lap, just as we have spent so many evenings in the past few weeks.

For me, the urgent requirement was to do my utmost to spend more time at home and I discussed it with the team at work who were enormously supportive of a potential plan to have say, Tuesday afternoons and Fridays at home, when I could work. Even though Roy may not be awake, it pleases him to have me around. I have done my best since then to shift my working day earlier so I get home earlier to spend what time I can here. The tension of this need is appalling, because the business requires my attention and from time to time I need to go away. I haven't managed to take any significant hours off, though.

We solved this particular problem in relation to my need to go to Newcastle for three or four days by hiring a car and Roy coming with me and our staying in Alnwick.

This expedition and our original plan to go to a large hotel in Whitley Bay where I had stayed frequently before and spent a good deal of money - including the first anniversary dinner for the business - prompted one of the most upsetting responses to our circumstances we experienced. I wrote to the hotel mentioning that I was being accompanied by a convalescent friend who would want to spend a good deal of his time in the hotel and asking, for example, what time it would be necessary to vacate the room each day for cleaning. The first response to this was a phone call from the wife of the proprietor asking some rather curious and direct questions about Roy's illness and claiming that it was necessary for her to know these things on the grounds of environmental health regulations. I gave very little away but told her that my companion was no risk to anyone and that it was simply a matter of having a change of air and some rest.

Very shortly after this, a single sentence fax was sent through to my office simply saying that the hotel was unable to accept the booking for my convalescing friend. The receptionist then phoned home, where I was, to explain that the fax had gone to work and to report the manager's decision. Having already received the fax at home by this time, I was in a state of purple fury about it, and the poor receptionist got the brunt of my anger and disgust - though I did make it clear that I was not addressing it to her but to the establishment. The incident profoundly upset me and I was contemplating all kinds of revenge on the hotel, which, in the event I have not had the time or energy to pursue. However, they remain on my priority list of those beyond forgiveness, and none of us has been near the place since. What was going on?

Our expedition to Alnwick and the business went really quite well. One evening we had dinner with Darren and Ian (members of the EQUUS team) and Ian's partner, Joanne, at the hotel and the following one with Tony

Kennan (my major client, and, as representative of the
major shareholder, fellow director) and his wife Maire.

Ian had been a member of Roy's team at London
Transport and he and Roy had become great friends. Roy
brought him home to dinner one evening (long before he was
ill) and he struck me as a very bright, energetic young man
whose talents were under-utilised at LT. I recruited him for
my then company (the one that eventually went into
liquidation). Much later he became one of the founding
shareholders of EQUUS, and ran our Newcastle office.

Some time after that first dinner he told me how nervous
he had been about spending an evening with 'the MD'-
someone as impressive as rumour suggested I must be. Ian
has since shown himself more than able to cope with people
of any degree of impressiveness.

When he first worked for me, the Company was
(amongst much else) running a Murder Mystery evening on
a riverboat on the Thames for a client. Ian and Roy were
togged up as our two representatives of the forces of law and
order - and both looked pretty stunning in their uniforms
amongst the murder victims, swag-carrying villains and
drunken party-goers. They'd both done a real security job
for us at a major open-air show in the north-east and were,
in any circumstance, brilliant at turning their hands to
anything that was needed.

Ian was just one of the many excellent people from all
walks of life whom Roy met and enjoyed and brought into
my life, to its great and continuing enrichment.

Tony Kennan is a long-time client, supporter, friend and
companion for me. While we spent relatively little real social

*time together, we have been involved in so many projects
and were in such constant communication that we came to
know and value each other intimately. He was one of a
small group of long-established clients who knew all about
our domestic situation and were as much at ease with it
as with their own.*

* * * *

Throughout this period, Roy has remained
extraordinarily calm, affectionate and sociable with only
occasional, short periods of depression - his cheerfulness,
affection, continuing gratitude and good spirits are an
astonishing testament to his courage and emotional
resources. He quite amazes me and all those who see
him.

From the beginning, he has been able to put up with
the discomforts and indignities of illness with a kind of
calm acceptance which remains astonishing.

There was one particular treat during this period.

We were both great fans of the comedienne Victoria
Wood, watching her TV shows, going to her live
performances and buying her videos. Her sense of
humour particularly tickled Roy, and was very similar to
his own. She gave us a lot of pleasure.

On the spur of the moment, when things weren't
looking too good, I wrote to her telling her about Roy's
condition and about how much he enjoyed her shows,
asking if she felt she could possibly pop in to see him. In
a phone call the next day from her office, her willingness
to visit was confirmed and a date was fixed.

All I told Roy a day or two before was that something important was happening on Friday and that he needed to be well. I told the medical team what was happening, that the drugs regime needed to be planned to ensure he was feeling good that day, and that they were not to call during the afternoon.

An hour or two before she was due to arrive, I told Roy who was coming and he clearly thought I was pulling his leg.

At the appointed time she arrived, much to Roy's astonishment and delight, and she spent an hour or so with us in comfortable, relaxing chat.

Roy's pleasure and incredulity were all I could have hoped for, and we were both thrilled and grateful that such a star could find time for us. Her visit said much about her quality. It was a touch of magic in dark times.

Our Christmas turned out to be a delight - all that we could ever have hoped for. Although working on Christmas Eve to the middle of the day, come Christmas Day the holiday mood took over and we slept until late, woke for a cup of tea and opening the presents, then back to sleep before a late afternoon Christmas dinner of goose and trimmings, all done in the comprehensively extravagant style of the household.

Roy had bought me the most wonderful range of exotic and lovely presents - bow-tie and necktie from Liberty, two pretty shaded candle-lamps and other lovely things - brilliant, wonderful presents which left me incredulous at his thoughtfulness and touched me deeply. How he got them or who bought them I don't know - it was just as if Father Christmas had visited.

On Christmas Day and Boxing Day we lazed about, watched television and videos way into the night, luxuriating in the freedom to do just as we pleased without external demands of any kind.

Our trip to Rotherham to Roy's mum in a hire-car the day after Boxing day went smoothly, though virtually from the moment we arrived till the moment we left, a day early, a succession of relatives and friends trooped through the door demanding attention and keen to see Roy. It was all far too much, too exhausting and we left earlier than we had expected longing for the peace and freedom of home.

Two and a half lovely, relaxed days over New Year again, though I was beginning to suffer some agitation in anticipation of the training project in the East Midlands which started at 9 o'clock on the first day back at work, Thursday 2 January.

While we had the hire-car, we accepted an invitation from Peter and Geraldine to go to their home in north London for afternoon tea, which was a delightful resumption of a more normal kind of life and a very pleasant occasion.

Since the new year, Iain and Jenny and the boys came for a Sunday afternoon tea which was, again, delightful, not least because they stayed just for three hours and, understanding our situation, did not impose themselves. (We are both very fond of the nephews and have had some excellent times with them - including the canal-boat week.) The following weekend Kevin and Liz from Doncaster came for Saturday evening and Sunday morning.

On the Saturday Roy and I had been into Balham to have his eye tested in the hope that some corrective lens could be provided to help him read a little more satisfactorily. The young optometrist was incredulous at the sight of Roy's devastated retina. We came home from that, he went to bed and in the evening he indicated that he would be happy to go out for a meal with Kevin and Liz so we went to the local wine bar, had a lot of wine and good food and returned home pretty merry. Shortly after returning home, Roy was sick. I think was as a result of the unusual exertions of the day and his body simply not being used to so much activity.

In the last week, we have had some anxious times with the reoccurrence of the diarrhoea and a continuing feeling of nausea with some vomiting.

The vomiting has been going on for some time now and the team have been trying to modify the medication to restore the balance after what had become a time of constipation, possibly prompting the vomiting. The balance tipped the other way and things looked as though they were beginning to get out of hand again but after a few days coming and going, alterations to the drugs, introduction of some new ones and so on, today, Saturday, we appear to be reasonably stable although he was sick once this morning.

About three weeks ago he developed a very unpleasant, infected rash in the middle of his pubic hair. A course of antibiotics seems to have reduced the infection and anti-fungal drugs have cleared up the rash considerably, though it is still far from healed. During the treatment of this, it seemed as though he had developed a small patch of KS (Kaposi's Sarcoma* - a typical cancer associated with

AIDS) in the same area which, though the doctors indicated was a matter of only slight concern or likely danger, is a fairly unnerving and worrying development - a further sign of the body's lack of resistance to attack, I think.

Apart from the constant state of anxiety about Roy's fundamental medical condition as well as the more superficial aspect of his daily comfort, the management of AIDS at home is immensely stressful. There have been times when the medical routines were enormously complicated and time-consuming, but even though they are now much simpler, they impose demands which have to be met irrespective of one's mood, energy or inclination. At the moment, the routine in the morning is the relatively simple one of disconnecting the overnight Hartmann's drip and attaching a bung to the line. In the evening, the syringe driver has to be made up (there have been times when this has involved eleven separate ampoules although it is now rather less), the potassium drip has to be made up and the Ganciclovir connected. Recently too, the rash has had to be bathed and dried.

Occasional episodes of vomiting or diarrhoea require psychological and practical response and there is a host of other simple, everyday demands which need to be met because, increasingly, he does not have the energy or motivation to attend to them. During the day there may be various communications to the medical team or information or instructions from them. Evenings and weekends we may be reporting on some slight change in circumstances to the medical team via the air call, discussing action with them, or there may be the fortnightly drugs list to write and deliver.

(I have a spreadsheet stock-list with about thirty items on it which I update with current requirements and drop into the GP's surgery on my way to work every two weeks.) Then the drugs and equipment to collect that evening - though we are fortunate to have the most wonderful pharmacist at the end of the road who has taken to delivering the large boxes of items we require. (I was always surprised to find myself walking home with enough diamorphine to put the entire local population on cloud 9!)

On some of the occasions when I have been able to get home early, the district nurses or the community care team member has been here and, again, that requires time and attention which fills the hours which might otherwise be free and relaxed. I am happy to do anything that will make him comfortable and will contribute to controlling the illness, but it is an unremitting and draining pressure. There are times when I wonder how I can continue to keep everything going.

There was one very strange period of a few weeks where I, certainly, was in a state of balance after we had 'cleared the decks' between us emotionally and prepared ourselves for death. Then the event for which we had prepared ourselves so thoroughly did not happen. Day to day it seemed almost as if we were simply waiting, that there was nothing else for us to do, nothing to keep us going, nothing to plan for. That period came to an end when we discussed it together and with the doctors, looking at the extraordinary question of 'permission to let go'. It's evident that in spite of such low energy, such little to look forward to, so little to hope for, Roy is not willing to give up, to let go yet.

Now, I think we regard each day as a gift which has to be taken as it comes; we have, to some extent, started thinking a little more about the short-term future - actively planning visits from friends, thinking of things we might do - even, today, talking about the possibility of booking our free TWA tickets to the West Coast of America - though both of us know, and Roy said, that the chances of our doing it are minimal. In respect of other things, our planning is much more low key but its resumption has taken us out of what was a rather gloomy waiting-room.

In spite of everything, perhaps because of it all, we are having times of the most extraordinary intimacy and affection without any hint of tension or difficulty between us. My desperate need is for occasional times to myself, quiet hours, away from the distraction of external events and demands and to know the ways in which I can make Roy more comfortable and comforted. He is really so undemanding personally, so accepting of the necessities of my life that he appears not to feel there is anything else which it is possible to give him or that he needs. I dearly hope that is the case, I do ask him, and I do not know if there is more we can do.

We were moved by Freddie Mercury's death. We watched the tribute programmes to him and our Queen videos feeling an extraordinary degree of identification and closeness with him, and admiration and pleasure in what he achieved.

We have also been watching the videotapes of the world trip and that has been lovely - not I think in any nostalgic, regretful way, but as an affirmation, a confirmation, a reminder of what we achieved against such odds.

It's the evening of Sunday 2nd February 1992. We've just come to the end of a disturbing and disturbed fortnight. The conclusion is probably that Roy has gone through a significant stage of deterioration and we must adjust ourselves once more to shortening perspectives.

It's disturbing how rapidly things move out of memory, developments which one would imagine would be etched in fire in one's brain. Time has been passing at such a speed, days have been so full, here and at work they are quickly dissolving into a single hazy past.

As things became slightly calmer, after bowels and stomach were a little more settled, we planned to go to Yorkshire, calling in at Roy's mum's, where he would stay when I went on to Newcastle for one night. The journey to Rotherham was pleasant, companionable and without problems and I set off early on the Monday morning for the north. During that day he had several episodes of diarrhoea and was, I think, sick once and was evidently feeling generally well below the levels of the previous weeks. I returned on the Tuesday evening, very late having driven through thick and freezing fog. He was welcoming and kindly as always, but evidently frail and under the weather.

The next day, Wednesday, we set out at about midday in quite bad fog, though nothing like the previous evening, and happily it cleared once we were out of Yorkshire.

I had already spoken to the community care team asking that we should have a 'ward round' as I felt that we needed to look at the whole situation and all the symptoms together and decide on a proper plan and adjust our expectations to the whole reality.

The journey home was easy and trouble-free and it was great to be back at home together with time for one of our quiet, companionable evenings dozing on the sofa in front of the TV.

On the Thursday, Anne-Louise paid a flying visit to look at the rash, his sinusitis and the numbness of the left half of his face which had recently begun. It was thought this might be associated with the sinusitis, though that hardly seemed to explain it.

On Friday afternoon I arrived home for the meeting with Anne-Louise and Vicky and it became evident that the sinusitis was actually much more serious than we had realised - a thick infection of the sinuses is difficult to clear, and with its proximity to the nervous system, major blood vessels and the brain is potentially very serious indeed. They prescribed a heavy arsenal of antibiotics to attack this, along with nasal drops to try and clear some of the passages.

With Anne-Louise and Vicky being air called and on and off the phone, we had several conversations in various combinations of the four of us, and it became clear that we probably had to accept a significant deterioration in Roy's condition with the particular threat of the sinus infection possibly spreading much more radically.

With the arrival of more tablets taking the daily total up to thirty or so, we organised to substitute some of them for injections to try and reduce the load.

When we had been reorganising the drug regime on the previous occasion and the number of daily tablets had risen to an intolerable level, several of them had been dropped, including the one thought possibly to have some effect on the cryptosporidium. Roy had said earlier this week that he had a feeling that his condition had deteriorated since that had stopped, so they listened and reinstated it. Being eight large tablets a day it considerably increased the burden of tablet-taking.

Within minutes of the medical team leaving on Friday, a potential new employee arrived for his interview and Roy retired to the back room to sleep. Having consumed a couple of bottles of wine and a brandy between the two of us once the formalities were over, I was pretty well-oiled by the time the now appointed candidate left. Roy was quite upset that on a day when such radical issues had been foremost in our minds, I could 'go off and get pissed'. I was in no state to justify my behaviour or respond sensitively to his distress, let the matter drop, and quickly it passed.

This was something profound and lasting I was taught by Roy - express feelings, get them out of the way and move on - lengthy analytical conversations (as were my habit) just kept things on the boil. The latter part of the evening, and the weekend resumed normal, quiet, friendly relations with no subsequent evidence of the first, tiny friction we have had between us for months. I have not yet addressed the bigger issues of Friday afternoon with him but need time to do so - when?

It's nearly one o'clock on Sunday night and we have just been through a lengthy evening routine following the Ganciclovir, four injections, connecting up the Hartmann's solution with the potassium, washing the rash, applying cream, and taking the nose drops. I fear that while the virulence of the rash is declining there is evidence of other unpleasant things happening, including possibly the arrival of more KS.

The sinuses seem to have loosened and eased a little today, and I just hope that he will have at least that relief, and recover some of the sensation in the left hand side of his face.

Tonight we sat and watched together our tape of the most beautiful programme about several American people of all kinds who are HIV positive and facing the crisis with incredible openness, courage, even humour. It was full of glorious things, including splendid statements about the huge strength of the gay community; the generosity and love shown between friends and lovers; the incredible strength and determination of people of all kinds, including a middle-aged married couple, a young newly-married couple and several others all coping with lives so much like our own. Roy watched and dozed and saw some of it.

I was encouraged to watch the tape by Roy's mum phoning up and saying she had seen it. It had evidently given her some food for thought and comfort - I think realising that what we were going through was just a tiny part of a global drama, not some isolated, squalid, regrettable, untypical private incident. It was a beautiful programme.

The DIARY

Part IV

March 1992

*A*t this stage, it was just two years since Roy's diagnosis and slightly less since PCP had arrived - the first identified symptomatic illness. His lungs were occasionally troublesome, but they had remained more or less stable with the infection held in check. The other invasions had progressively weakened him as their effects accumulated and accelerated: CMV had led to blindness in his right eye and was eating away at the retina of his left; cryptosporidium in his stomach and gut subverting the whole digestive system with permanent, underlying diarrhoea; infected open sores and small patches of skin cancer in the groin; progressive numbness in the left side of his face where the original infection in the sinuses had taken hold and spread to affect the facial nerves.

These were the things we knew about; what other infections, if any, were working away unnoticed, or what other effects the known infections were having, we didn't know. What we did know was, that in the effort to control the known infections and to boost his immune system, gallons of vicious chemicals had been poured into his bloodstream, and kilograms of unforgiving tablets had been in and out of his stomach. While there was some evidence of cause and effect in particular treatments and their results - most obvious in the impact of Pentamadine on PCP, in the palliative drugs, the steroids and the magical effect of morphine on chronically uncontrollable bowels - much of the process was uncertain and experimental. We had no idea if the chemo-therapy actually inhibited the progress of CMV in his eyes; massive doses of broad-spectrum antibiotics sometimes had positive effects on suspected, unidentified infections, sometimes not; whether or not AZT influenced the progress of HIV was not apparent (though the unpleasant side-effects were all too clear).

What the medical team were able to do with remarkable skill was symptom-management, sometimes, by their own admission, using wildly unconventional, high-risk methods. With relatively little concern for anything beyond the short to medium term (and in the last months, only the very short-term), they could manipulate the drug regime and target a special day or week (or, early on, as much as a month in the case of the world trip) and provide Roy with a reasonably comfortable, limited period of strength when it was a priority for him.

But they were as surprised as anyone by the constant unpredictability of his physical condition: the repeated, sudden plunges into apparently final decline; the equally rapid revivals to brightness and strength. For these there was no rationale at all: at times it must simply have been remission of the infectious assault; at others Roy's indomitable spirit and the life force within him. We were to see more of this extraordinary process even in the face of death.

While the good periods were a cause of rejoicing, they could not disguise the gradual ebbing of strength and life from his frail and damaged body. Now, in March 1992, the end was drawing nearer, though it was not at all to be the process we had envisaged - inasfar as we had envisaged anything clearly. It was to be both more complex and more beautiful than we could ever have imagined, and both of us became acquainted with aspects of being which were exceptional and mysterious.

It was also to be a time of chaos and panic and mess. Mystery was the last thing in our minds as we struggled with the all-too physical reality of a body in its last, wretched struggles. But mystery there was, and peace, too, even amidst such disorder.

* * * *

1 March Sunday: After preparing ourselves for the worst before Christmas, we've been given more time - much more - than the medical team expected. Much of it has been positive and delightful. Roy has maintained that cheerful, generous spirit through many real trials.

This last weekend, I went very near the edge - inner chaos, sleeplessness for a night, a day of disorientation and low productivity. I think it was all to do with energy and stress - too little of the former, too much of the latter.

At a time when the business has been dodgy - though not in crisis - and we're still not profitable - when there are three redundancies completed or in hand - when there isn't enough business to see us through to the future - the demands at home, the early mornings, late nights - all with the complex medical routines - have sapped my vital energy. I can manage the public performances perfectly - lectures, training and presentations round the country - but very quickly tire.

There is also the profound, intense problem of endings - as I prepare myself for the most radical ending of my life, it is very hard to live and believe in continuity - especially of the business which is not as healthy as it should be: can I find the drive, optimism, direction for it while I prepare for death? How's that conflict affecting my feeling, thinking, performance in ways I can't recognise?

I had long talk with Rob (palliative care consultant) and Vicky (palliative team community care nurse) the other evening while Roy slept: they offered respite - one day's medical routines carried out by someone else, for example; they offered the liberation of expressing my feeling of weakness. I find it difficult to think of giving up the nursing - in however small a measure - as it's so deeply - automatically - instinctively? - identified with my commitment to Roy. Rob rightly said it's the uncertainty which is debilitating - particularly the uncertainty of how long I have to find the resources to carry on for. The conversation was a relief - it's given me strength and some clarity about where I must go - at work for example. I think I also felt I could carry on a bit longer afterwards.

We also talked about my rage at the district nurse's Christian missionary activities in the sickroom. (One day she had read or sung hymns to him when he was comatose and I was at work.) Rob and Vicky admitted (to my intellectual astonishment) that their purpose in work was to 'bring about the kingdom of God' - but they acknowledged the vital issue of patients' freedom of choice and that their aims remained private and invisible.

There's a strange paradox - at the point of vulnerability approaching death, people are bound to be susceptible to comforting images and prospects - relatively defenceless; but, also, at that point there is (it has to be admitted) also unique confrontation with issues which may have been exhaustively resolved during health, but which now take on a quite different aspect. I pointed out that part of my objection was to the sectarian approach (naive Christianity) - when there were thousands of faiths or systems of thought and values, any one of which might offer comfort or glimpses of a greater truth. It was not part of my deal with the local health centre that one quaint faith should be introduced into the sickroom. I wrote a furious letter which didn't get sent.

It's been a very tough time - for Roy too as he finds less energy, fewer days when he's feeling relatively well.

But we continue peacefully and companionably to watch TV, videos, snooze together, eat well - and enjoy the prospect and reality of eating (it's still one of the things which brings a brightness to his face - cakes especially!)

He's fed up, as he says, with 'people mauling his groin' - and getting through the cleaning routine three times a day as prescribed is painful and difficult.

6 March: It seems certain that he is dying, and likely that he will go very soon, this weekend, they say. I feel eerily reconciled, ready. Rob has just left - after another of those extraordinary conversations flying from the potent reality of Roy sleeping above us to the grand issues of life, death,

meaning, quality of life and all the rest - and back again. Rob is a philosopher and has the depth and breadth - and empathy - to help throw light on the most abstruse of thoughts and inklings. Emotionally I could never have coped without his wisdom and support; intellectually and spiritually I would never have covered such ground as was possible with him and Vicky.

The time is precious. He is sleeping, deeply sedated. He's woken a few times when I've been to see him - comfortable it seems after the headache of this morning and of yesterday, and the sickness. He wanted nothing - just towels to cover the pillow and over him while he sweated.

He has kept his life, his spirit to the end - AIDS has not diminished that lovely being - though his body has suffered and declined he's remained gentle, affectionate - and - oh dear! grateful. Such greatness of spirit. What a guy.

Detail is so precious - it can never come again - to hold onto what has been so rich - terrible and lovely a period. Between us there has been such harmony, such intimacy, such affection, closeness, that it has been wonderful - not even, but especially those many dozy evenings on the sofa - his hand seeking mine - us both half asleep, still, together.

7 March Saturday: We slept well - me after a couple of sleeping pills, Roy peacefully - with the unnerving, drug-induced breathing pattern Rob predicted - ten to fifteen seconds silence between each exhalation before resuming.

This morning he's been quite peaceful - awake for minutes at a time and pretty coherent - just the edge of confusion about time, day, telephone (does it work?)

and so on. We decided we would not tell his mum about the position, but he wanted to call her and sister and family later on. We agreed we'd see it through here, together, with a few of our friends.

I cried this morning, holding his hand. He said again - as he said so often - 'I don't feel any different' - still aware of all the possibilities of life, knowing he hasn't the strength.

I said he was to let me know of anything at all he wanted - however extravagant - if he wanted to talk to the captain of the QE2, I'd phone him. He replied: 'Just the little miracle man who can replace all the bits.'

He said, 'I don't want to be alone,' and I promised that he wouldn't be. He wanted me with him.

I have to face the working week - how many of the days can I take off? We'll see. Hour by hour. We'll see about tomorrow, Sunday, and then Monday.

It's the strangest time - quiet, peaceful, yet emotionally charged: tears are not far away. He has not cried.

One aspect of all this - unexpected, bizarre - is that the time of death seems dependent, quite substantially, on external factors - the assessment of the medics ('Is it now or soon?') - their clinical reaction to things (withdrawal of antibiotics, abandoning the regime of drugs) - and on me (and them) curiously nudging him towards the final moment - Rob would call it giving Roy 'permission' to go - I have to believe it's helpful - the alternative (perhaps) is his lingering, deeply sedated - but to what purpose for him? (Life is precious, letting go an anxious and frightening decision - perhaps we need to help, reassure, comfort, even hasten the moment.) Rob suggested that I should say that I really have to go to work on Monday - perhaps it would help Roy to slip away this weekend - to take the hint, to spare me the trouble, I suppose. It's not an easy idea to live with if it's not absolutely right for Roy. Can we ever be sure what is right for him?

Though sleepy and sleeping much, he is still so thoughtful: asking for orange juice this morning he said I was to shower and dress beforehand, it could wait.

(Sue's with him now - he asked her if she'd like a cup of tea. We made one for him. She was telling me about the time he was hooked up to the Ganciclovir drip hung from the chandelier downstairs and still asked if he could get her anything! He has always been - and remains - so beautifully altruistic.)

Slowly, since yesterday (Friday when I worked effectively until 7pm) all affairs outside the house are receding - even work is beyond serious thought at the moment - I ask myself if I want to go on with it at all - it's all been so much devoted to keeping our house and life afloat and finances liquid and free from worry - without Roy I should perhaps be doing something less strenuous! Though, I dare say, I shall be glad of the distraction and the discipline.

He was deeply asleep for hours into the night. I sat with him holding his hand, expecting him to die any moment. What would it be like? Would I recognise the moment, would I know for sure? Eventually I slipped into bed with him - watching, listening, expecting every breath to be his last. Then I fell asleep.

Sheer willpower - that's what's kept him going.

8 March Sunday: Well, what a disorienting switch-back of emotions! Today he is bright, lively, chatty, lighthearted - Roy as of old - hardly dopey from drugs - eating and drinking, bright-eyed. It's absolutely knocked me for six after the death-watch by his bed yesterday - it's been a delight, but at the same time - having, yesterday, just about adjusted myself - and at the boundaries of emotional, imaginative energy - I hardly know what to do now. As I write (6pm - he's sleeping after Terry's visit and scrambled egg, toast, milk) I feel that I can hardly face the outside world and its demands at all - I want it all to go away for good. Reading about Anthony Powell in the Sunday paper - a leisurely life with money behind him - I just longed for peace and freedom. I am facing, in full knowledge, what I imagine goes on in the heads of those who have nervous breakdowns - it's all just too much. I feel very close to incompetence, impotence.

The business needs prime energy and leadership - now more than ever I've got to be on the ball, up to the minute - and I just don't feel I can cope with it. I shall have to. There's so much at stake - yet, in my heart of hearts, now, I can't be bothered with it. I wait for a miracle - an order for 20,000 of the books; the huge contract offering immediate pay-off - my fantasy life is actually more of the collapse and liquidation variety - it's so hard to separate home and away - home's perspectives are hours or days - and inevitable ending - how can I feel and act at work in a perspective of optimistic weeks, months, years?

It's all very hard - and in spite of all the support and help we've got - no one can lift the burden.

10 March: Two more days of comfort, good spirits, much sleep - after Sunday's hours of unexpected sunshine. Sunday and Monday evenings he struggled downstairs and snacked, drank, watched TV (though he can see very little now) and then launched himself back upstairs. On Sunday he agreed that he didn't mind my going to work - he'd prefer to be alone than have strangers in the house. Monday had a comforting blanket bath from nurse Cathy. Terry's lilies blooming and pouring sweet scent into the room.

This evening - Nicky visited - Roy ate a little - tottered (quite competently) to the loo - satisfactory visit followed by strip wash on his own. Back to bed - good humour - moments of abstraction - that smile ever available. In the end he didn't get downstairs - left too late - but he's in good form. Wants his Ganciclovir done tonight. All exhaustingly well!

14 March Saturday: Apparently quite stable up to yesterday - very sleepy, but lucid periods between sleeps. Thursday and Friday evenings he struggled down for a few hours - painfully slowly - taking ages to shift from lying, ages to stand up - waiting for strength and circulation to return to his legs, and then slow progress, holding my arm to the top of the stairs. He came down on his own, with me just a couple of steps ahead. He was comfortable, propped up on extra cushions on the sofa - ate (fruit salad, Yorkshire biscuits and tea last night) while we watched Victoria Wood and Educating Rita. Back upstairs was a tremendous struggle for him - bent forward, grasping both bannisters, panting once he'd got to the top - but he implicitly refused any substantial assistance. Even turning in bed, getting up on an elbow to have a drink is a huge effort.

Tuesday and Wednesday at home for me were relatively easy - I got a lot of EQUUS things done at home (though energy started to fail in the afternoon) and then there was the awful problem of deciding about Thursday and Friday. The prospect of being 'out there' again and away from him put me into a complete dither - should I/shouldn't I go? Should I/shouldn't I keep the appointment in Manchester? I phoned Ben to cancel Friday - but no reply - then I talked it over with Roy (he didn't get up that evening) and he said I was to go and get on with things. His strength and clarity allowed me to do so. On Thursday I was surprisingly clear-headed and purposeful at work, and the trip to the North West went well - I knew the district nurses would be in twice, and I phoned three times - Roy on each occasion sounding very strong and clear.

Today there seems to have been a change. While we were both still in bed he said he felt sick, and prepared himself two or three times. He wasn't. At about 11 I got up and gave him intravenous dexamethasone and other drugs while he remained apparently asleep. Since then - up to 4pm or so - he's not really woken up - no response to voice, even with eyes open - and no hand pressure in response to mine. Nicky and nurse Cathy came. I couldn't rouse him. Then a few minutes of being awake - remembering nothing of the day so far - wanted cold orange, help with turning over (such a struggle for him) and back to sleep. I sat with him, then fell asleep myself. The appearance is that he is slipping away - but he's fooled us plenty of times before!

Last night, after we'd been watching TV (although having drawn up the syringe for the driver and got the Ganciclovir in the room early in the evening - I completely forgot both until about 11pm) - by the time we started moving (around midnight) I was so tired I wondered how I was going to be able to get through the duties - helping him up, undressing, drawing up syringes, making his hot water bottle - an hour's worth - but eventually it was done. I took a couple of sleeping tablets and slept soundly. (I've taken them three or four out of the last seven nights I think.)

There are awful moments - often quite unexpected: I got back from shopping sometime in the last week - and as I came through the front gate, I felt how it would be returning to an empty house; I hover between wishing it were all over - and absolute delight at his continuing, substantial psychological presence - he has moments - longer periods too - when he's so full of spirit, good humour, so much himself - his smile, his kindness, his (again!) gratitude.

I don't believe he's shown a moment of anger or irritability for weeks - though I think he did tell the district nurse off yesterday for being too rough and boisterous when she was washing him! We joke about the two of them - old-fashioned bossy boots as they both are! But they're kindly and efficient and well-intentioned.

I've said to one or two friends this week - and it's a powerful feeling - that everything else in the world seems trivial and inconsequential outside this house - outside Roy's room. I've had several moments of euphoric imagining how things would be without the pressure and tension of external demands - a little country retreat, a career as a writer, setting my own pace and goals, having a secure income without all the anxiety and pressure. I thought about resigning from the business - selling up, disappearing. Obviously I've not done anything about it - but I know I don't have the energy - and available optimism - that work needs. I'm doing everything necessary - and (to my amazement) doing much of it very well I think - drawing on that great reservoir of skill, experience, knowledge - the brain functioning (almost on auto-pilot) remarkably when the circumstances and stimuli are right.

As I write now, I wonder about all this scribble - what use will it be - will I ever want to, or have the patience to make anything of it? I'm so much of an improviser in some ways - seat of the pants stuff so often (though often inspired too!) that I may not have the patience to process so many pages.

Writing now is something to do with not wanting to lose any of this - this huge, unique, extraordinary, awful reality - not to lose anything while he still lives and breathes in the room above me, because life is soon to change with such drama. I do not feel it will be the end of the world - there's even a sense of the likely relief - the opening of horizons - once it's over - I do not feel guilty about that, for I would profoundly prefer it not to happen at all - but my world has shrunk to this tiny, physical compass, to this vast, resonant, gloomy, sad prospect - and I am longing for wider horizons again.

But what I shall do emotionally without him, I simply don't know. Our relationship has been so rewarding, so harmonious, so influential - he has changed me - so many of the ways I react, feel - act (even down to cleaning up in the kitchen when I cook!) - much of it in ways I can only glimpse occasionally. He has such an uncorrupted character in many ways - direct, spontaneous, lacking (I think) the complex, labyrinthine emotional inner life that has been my reality - not that he's not complex, but it's a complexity lived with ease, with simplicity, I think. Our feelings and reactions have become so very close in so many areas over the years - differences resolved happily - quite a contrast to the few conflicts and battles we had early on - rare as they were.

That closeness has borne lovely fruits over the period of his illness, I think - especially recently when I have felt our intimacy without barriers - often without words - intensely. I require nothing from him - what he is and what he gives is wonderfully enough.

He seems at peace, too, I don't feel that there's anything he feels I should be or should be doing more than I am.

In the most heroic vein he has been fighting this plague with all his huge reserves of energy and determination. When I've mentioned it, he's said words to the effect, 'Well, you've got to!' and his struggle to get out of bed, at cost of such effort, is a daily, extraordinary demonstration of what is huge moral and physical strength.

Today it looks as though even that energy is waning fast.

The peace between us has also, I think, been peaceful reconciliation to reality - he's not reconciled to the act or decision of letting go - he's not willing to die - may never reach that point - but to the fact that he will soon die, we are both reconciled.

I do not know whether I should be sitting by him the entire time, or getting on with things around the house - including this record - but I feel I need to keep doing - though returning to him every thirty or forty minutes. Last weekend showed me the intense, all absorbing cul-de-sac which awaits - and I can't risk going back into that. He knows I'm close by.

The shrinking of horizons, and adaptation to them has been a remarkable process. The community care team have talked a good deal about this with us - the issue of quality. The most dramatic decision was in the autumn when we agreed to the starting of steroids - knowing that the cost might be in terms of less time, but the benefit being better quality. And quality was delivered generously.

There have been several 'moves of the goalposts' to shorter perspectives since then - until now it is just an hour or two a day when he is even conscious and when what he has is no more than absence of gross pain, me and some sense of physical and psychological comfort.

Prior to this stage the daily area of quality was simply getting up when I came home, eating together (and how precious those meals were - usually pretty good stuff, some full roast meals, with Marks and Spencer luxuries of various sorts) - though sometimes he'd eat little or nothing (I hoped he'd eat but didn't mind if he didn't, however elaborate the meal), settling down in front of the TV together and him snoozing most of the time - that was an oasis of quality to which he was quite reconciled. Now, it's so much less, but I think it's been OK.

I suppose I'm obsessed with writing about all this because I feel nothing so intense or important is ever likely to happen again - that it is the single, most vivid and intense experience of my life - that it is valuable, beautiful, terrifying - bringing us - together - in the company of issues and feelings which one can hardly expect ever to imagine.

Also, of course, I feel that in the end, I shall have to - want to - write about it: perhaps out of this tragedy I shall be able to create an inspiring memorial - to Roy, his heroism, our love, for those who are facing the same drama.

It changes one's perspectives, yet again! - on suffering and death - how can we permit people to suffer so much - to visit on others voluntarily the pain and grief we have had imposed on us or to neglect its relief?

I've just been up to look at him. A brief fluttering into consciousness. 'Are you alright?' he asks me. There is nothing he wants. His eyes close. A slight knitting, frowning of the brows - a passing, disturbing image or memory. He does not look absolutely at peace, but he does not look troubled.

16 March Monday: Yesterday was a bad day for me - feeling disoriented, depressed, fragile. I mooched about achieving less than enough (whatever enough might be), dabbled with a piece of pessimistic writing about the human race - but was comforted by the registrar late in the evening who, sensing my trouble, prescribed whisky and sleeping tablets.

Later on, Roy had urgent loo call - panic! - slight accident - bulk OK on the commode - but I feared my handling of him wasn't too effective or gentle. Second alarm at 7am today - made it to the commode, but again, difficult, awkward. He can't be left on his own!

11pm: Tried to work at home today - lots of interruptions, distractions - district nurse in the morning, learning to lift Roy, incontinence equipment, changing sheets. Reassuring volunteer co-ordinator phoned - volunteer Dennis turned up - reassuring, competent too - colleague from work came for meeting - consultant, trainee nurse and district nurse arrived - whirlwind activity - Roy out of bed - on the commode - bed sheets changed - new comfy, medical mattress in place - washed, cleaned - commode emptied and cleaned.

Roy's just said he couldn't believe how many people there'd been and how much going on: 'You standing in the middle of the whirlwind scratchin' your head!' he said to me.

All movement is uncomfortable now - all's fine when he's still - but turning, drinking, all major operations. Very tiring. I thought I'd reached the edge with medical routines

- now all this - and (bliss!) five hours a day to go out to work while volunteer sits in. Oh dear.

And he's had a headache today he didn't mention and I didn't know about.

17 March Tuesday 11:45pm: A frightening day! Late last night I was whacked - had a couple of small whiskies and two sleeping tablets and went to bed. 3am - ouch! - Roy needs underwear, etc., changing. I don't think I was very gentle or kind - I don't really remember - except being panic-stricken about the effect on the next day's work. It took about an hour.

Woken at 6:50 by Roy in same position again. I was in a bad way emotionally - there's something very oppressive about shit - not the substance - but the meaning, the difficulty of the routine (removing nappies, knickers with Roy's weight on half the mess), the slow, risky removal trying to prevent leakage, the evidently upsetting effect on Roy of the physical movement and harassment.

I managed to shower and have some breakfast before colleague from work arrived at about 9am.

Earlier, Roy had said he wanted to phone his mum, sister and niece - he felt the time was getting close.

This is the first time he's been so explicit. I took that as a serious indication of change - of imminent change. We discussed if I was to go out while the volunteer sat in - yes, Roy said. 'You'll hang on for me?' I said. 'Yes,' he said.

I phoned the community care team and reported in. Said I was going out for my five hours to put my world in order and get back here permanently. As the day progressed that resolve hardened. At work I went through everything - I think very clear-headedly - and left at 2:30pm feeling there weren't any loose ends and that things were in strong capable hands. Irrespective of Roy's condition tomorrow I'm staying at home for as long as it takes now.

I lay on the bed with him for a few hours after I got home - then best part of four hour's nursing. One accident - I phoned community care team for advice - just got that cleaned up and new knickers on, when another - much looser and more threatening. Agreed to leave him as he was for a little time in case there was more.

Returned, cut knickers off, re-equipped and settled - almost immediately he thought he was going to go again. Didn't, much to my relief. I was beginning to be very hot and weary. Several sessions of dripping water into his mouth with a toothbrush, then a drink of orange. Got him to sign get well card for his mum and birthday card for sister. He talked to them both on the phone. One or two odd hallucinations for me: 'Must I get up and go to work?' - plus one or two other secret frights which had no words.

Thank god I'm not going to work - I'm only just keeping myself together - physically even more than emotionally.

Roy seems quite peaceful. I asked him if he felt it was coming close. 'Yes, a feeling.' Was he frightened of anything. 'No.' Good news.

18 March Wednesday-Midnight: This chap is continually incredible. After a day of almost completely unconscious, he's just asked to sit on the edge of the bed for a drink. Lifted up by my newly learnt nurse's hold, he

sat up (initially several empty retches - alarmingly) and then drank one and a half glasses of orange and half a glass of water. (He'd drunk very little from glasses or cups for some time, needing all liquids dripped into his mouth.)

We had the most sustained chat for a long time (intermittent for ten minutes) - about nurses, volunteers, my plans - not going to work - at which he said, 'You're not going to let it jeopardise the business?' - I reassured him. The brain - the generous Roy - is still in there, active and alive.

Then he suggested that they might give him supplementary feeding through the Hickman line - those huge bags with the beeping machine on the drip stand. Well! I asked him if he'd changed his mind from yesterday (about time being short). He said you couldn't tell. (Burst of inner turmoil for me - how much longer?)

It's been a bad day for me - woke up with headache and feeling groggy - didn't improve till after one and a half hour's sleep this afternoon while volunteer sat in and watched Roy.

Volunteer Dennis was splendid this morning - Roy already needed changing when he arrived, then he did the most enormous, forceful pee which soaked right up to his chest in the sheets. Dennis and I between us changed everything - me lifting Roy onto his feet briefly - then all fresh and comfortable. It would not have been possible on my own.

Roy finds one of the district nurses a discomforting person - she's not gentle he says and doesn't do what he says - he didn't want washing and she washed him!

I've spent much of the (pottering) day looking through all our photos to find a selection of ones of Roy to mount for the funeral. I've also decided it will be a champagne buffet, fifty candles, flowers - an occasion to celebrate his life and courage. At the present rate, however, the plans will be on ice indefinitely! He's so weak and sleepy, yet there's a dynamo at work inside. He knows just what he wants and when he wants time to decide what he wants, and is quite clear. He's also so appreciative - in an ordinary, generous, courteous way - 'Please' every time, or, 'Well done!' or, 'Oh! Well done!' on occasions (a successful and comfortable lift for example). He succumbs willingly to the routines - turning - 'It's time to turn,' I say; 'OK,' he says.

He seems to be almost totally blind in his left eye now as well - says he can't see my face - can't see any difference when the main light's put on. Can just see moving hand directly in front of face. Poor guy. He's not complaining - though last night asked if we couldn't stop the diamorphine, I think so that he could be more alert (he's on half a gram a day (enough to zap an elephant) and it makes him very woozy). Blindness was always what he feared most - yet now he is living with it peacefully. Oh my, what strength; what drama!

Being off work has been a great relief - though I've really not been well enough to enjoy it. There are lots of resources on hand - volunteer overnight, etc. - they're a remarkable bunch.

19 March Thursday It's 5:30am - an hour and a half after I woke to find Roy with the covers turned down looking for his glass of drink (at the very passive stage of looking - he had the intention). He then said he needed to go to the loo. Debate about commode or not. Agreed too much trouble - and too risky getting there. Agreed to get on with it. Checked pads etc. Covered him up. He looked very unhappy, 'Very embarrassing,' he said it was - eyes screwed shut, holding my hand. It was a huge, very liquid stool which flooded out round his buttocks and settled like a little lake. I was inwardly appalled. Suggested getting on-call team nurse. Roy said he'd rather we did it. He was very practical and clear. So we set about it slowly and methodically and with his active co-operation - first, staying absolutely still, then moving from side to side, completed the whole operation in about forty minutes or so - powdered, dressed and clean. It was a miracle the bed didn't get soiled.

Then it was time for a drink. Lift, and up onto the edge of the bed (we've got this one sorted now!). Glass of orange and back to sleep for him; tea and diary for me. I feel fine - calm, practical, alert. We've had an amusing and agreeable exchange - matter of fact about immediate requirements, whimsical about a tequila sunrise and special barman for Mr Deakin (he asked for the same one he had last time - who let him 'cling on' while he was drinking). Roy entered the spirit of things beautifully. It's noticeable how quickly he's adapted to loss of sight by using his hands to feel for things and check. He never forgets the syringe driver or the bowl by his side. Still, in the midst of mess and indignity, calm and warm and kindly.

I do wonder how long this will continue. We must get the medication sorted out - this routine is no fun for either of us - but the alternative may be masses of diamorphine and much deeper sedation. I don't really want that when he's in such good humour - it would be sad for him not to be able to express it and for me not to enjoy it.

Thursday midnight: this guy is amazing. These snippets - him having just gone blind, knowing he's dying:

BH: I'm just going round the bed.

RD: Just going round the bend?

BH: Oh! I've been there for years.

RD: F T. No comment.

or,

RD: The orange is odd. What kind is it?

BH: Robinson's whole orange.

RD: It's a bit odd.

BH: I'll write to Mr Robinson and tell him his orange is odd.

RD: Cricket's cancelled.

BH: Why's that?

RD: The orange is off.

- all with a cheeky smile on his lips - poor lips that are so dry he has to have paraffin wax on them so that he can get a grip on the straw.

A very busy day for visitors! Registrar, GP, district nurse arrived just after two volunteers had left - slight bedlam!

Medical review suggested putting up diamorphine to 700mg per day (it's been 500 for ten days or so); Buscopan stays at 120mg (up recently from 60, then 100 because of diarrhoea); Nozinan up to 37.5 (last three days or so); and Midozolam 5mg all in syringe driver. Some bleeding from the KS in his groin today. Mid-afternoon, had good sit up on edge of bed session - lots of orange and good pee into bottle - fresh knickers, good lift - good partnership! I'm learning to help him keep track of the days - I always say, 'It's five o'clock on the afternoon of Thursday' - or whatever - he's getting his sense of night and day back a little. Also helping him cope with not seeing anything - warning him of drink approaching, guiding his hand to tissues and bowl, etc.

I've been giving him most of his drink with a straw - just picking up two inches or so, stopping top with finger and releasing it into his mouth - much better than toothbrush, though that worked well. We've got this down to an almost wordless routine now - he opens his mouth and sticks out his tongue (as I said to him like a baby bird waiting for mummy coming home with food!) and I deliver the orange. When he's had enough he moves his hand from side to side.

Seeing him not seeing (his left eyelid is hardly opening over his now sightless eye, recently his good eye) has brought me close to tears - it's awful - the thing he feared most - yet there's so little sign of distress, though registrar felt it was upsetting him this morning.

I realised in a flash of inspiration early this morning that we've been treating him as incontinent - which he's not - he's just immobile. 'Bedpans!' I demanded. None to be had - Boots? - 'Two days to three weeks,' they said. Useless. Then, of course, bloody hell, there's actually a bedpan in the commode so we'll try that next. I feel so stupid.

New district nurse turned up today in uniform - I opened the door and looked blankly at her (no finesse some nurses - she obviously thought it was obvious who she was). I mentioned that she was the first person in the whole medical team who'd turned up in uniform and let the street know what was going on. 'Did I mind?' she asked. I wasn't sure if I did or not. 'I never thought,' she said - a little lapse, I think - the district nurses are the least sophisticated of all the medical team - they're competent, dedicated professionals, but tending to a slightly overbearing, jollying kind of behaviour. One of them is the only person who's made me feel at all inadequate or criticised - she has an unconscious and unrecognised assumption that I'm stupid or ignorant. The example which sticks out was when she saw the Flagyl infusion. She picked up a sterile swab and said, 'When you draw this up you must use one of these...' Well, of course, I had been using them for weeks. (It was rather remarkable to discover that some of our daily routines even nurses aren't allowed to do because of the radical nature of the drugs and procedures.) There was also the Christian bit too, about which I still feel very uneasy and upset. I'm in danger of getting obsessed by the issue - but in the midst of all this stress, these things matter. What matters more is that Roy feels one or two of them handle him roughly and wash him (or whatever) whether he wants it or not. They are a bit bull-in-a-china-shoppish in comparison with the laid-back community care team.

Roy has been remarkable. Sue visited today and his first question was, 'How is Snooks?' (her cat).

I've been thinking a good deal about the funeral today - writing words, ordering the pictures, and so on. It's odd - but it seems to be necessary - it's got to be good and planning is essential.

20 March - Friday midnight: A really most pleasing day with regard to Roy's condition - though an utterly paralysing one from my point of view - hours and hours of nursing.

I was up around 9 (having provided drinks for him around 6) - and wasn't finished until 12 - drinks, experiment with bedpan (he didn't need it after all but good practice!) - then district nurse, then real need for bedpan, then clearing up, drinks, mouthwashes, injections - etc. etc. Volunteer came at 1pm - I went shopping, bought electric bell to summon the staff, as I told him - his voice is too weak to shout (though it looks as though it may just be too difficult for him even to press the little button). District nurse, then friend Nicky came, then 9:30 - drink - he got himself up on the edge of the bed - the commode - are we making progress or are we making progress?!!! When I went to get fish and chips (our Chinese next-door neighbours run the fish and chip shop at the end of the road) he ordered a variety of fizzy drinks - asked for cream soda and ice cream - gulped it down, belched, apologised and said, 'I'm enjoying it so much!' and then had another glassful. To be able to find such pleasure! There were tears of joy in my eyes.

He's been full of strength, endurance, goodwill today - amazing - humour. Talking about how the district nurse had been much better today, he said it resulted from her being told what's what - 'I'm becoming like you,' he said to me, 'a - Friesian!' I said, 'Well, you shouldn't have to put up with such things.' He said, 'But some things are beyond your control.' Indeed.

My, my, it's demanding work - he has no sense of time at all - time of day, or duration - our last session was over an hour and a half - and I was whacked - he couldn't remember when he'd been on the commode - just forty minutes earlier.

He's still so kind and grateful - and affectionate - the hand proffered for holding, the generous word.

He's obsessed with the bowl by his side - hating the prospect of being sick without it. Bedpan and commode are a great relief to him, I think. His sense of the most basic dignity and order.

21 March Saturday 6am: Up since 5 when Roy woke me saying he needed the loo. We managed bedpan routine very efficiently together and cleared up in a total of only about twenty minutes. Then drinks - first from straw (drink bombs!) - then from 20ml syringe - works much better.

I put talc on after I had dried him: 'Executive!' he says, 'I'll come here again!'

It's a wild, windy, wet morning - dawn chorus surprisingly vigorous outside - he can't hear it.

For the physical movements he counts down and then makes the move - wherever possible on his own - e.g., shunting the few inches up the bed after he's been sitting on the edge before lying down again, '5-4-3-2-1.'

I think I may prepare the morning drugs injections now - then we can sleep in without worry.

He's very coherent - just occasional wanderings as what's going on in his head becomes words - but not much - once or twice he's alarmed me by startled physical movement as he's tried to get up or do something - but easily dissuaded.

I must get back - he's back on the pan for a possible second bout.

11:15pm: We woke at 11ish - Roy very dry mouth - I pottered about, came back in and found him flat on his back doing arm exercises: 'Just to keep things moving,' he said.

There is something quite alarming about the unreserved demands - demands made absolutely on inner promptings and needs without regard for normal constraints.

We've just had an (endless) two and a half hour session - starting with a succession of drinks - ginger beer, cream soda, lemon squash and, second time round, water, milk and finally tea. There was a bedpan session - excellent, swift, efficient, all cleared up, then a slight accident - new pads, cleaned up - OK - more drink - then another call - largish wet one - cleaned up, new knickers - more drink - sit up on edge of bed - change syringe driver - evening injections.

There was a point at which the demands were beginning to wear me thin - grate on my nerves - five drinks in a row (down to kitchen, new glass, more ice, back up) - it felt as if it could go on forever until I simply passed out. He's very gentle, appreciative in his requests - and has no sense whatever of my exhaustion, nor the time and energy he's demanding.

I missed three TV programmes I thought I might escape into - they're all taped - and now I sit dreading the next call. I was thinking how potent a drama this relationship is - how it could be a kind of nightmare play or novel, in which the weak, helpless patient destroys the healthy, living carer completely and unwittingly.

I think there are few barriers between his internal world and the external now. He comes out with odd remarks which belong to the internal world, which make little sense:

'Fifteen quid's a lot for the fare.'

'Where to?' I say.

'Milton Keynes and that place up there on the wall.'

(He points to a map he can see.)

'You're looking at a different wall,' I say.

'No, that one there,' he points ahead as if it existed outside his head.

(Milton Keynes is the rail station we travel to when visiting my brother.)

Or,

'It's just a single track in London...'

'Railway or underground?' I hazard (this one peters out).

There are times (there were a couple tonight) when I feel so detached from him himself - when he seems to be a kind of insatiable object or machine - where imperatives follow each other so rapidly it's extraordinary. Three bedpan sessions in a row - it's hard to remain patient and kind - I manage it - but each occasion is a swallowing of exhaustion, a denial of hopes to sit down mindlessly and watch TV, have a fag and a cup of tea.

It looks as though the diarrhoea is as controlled as it's going to be - we'll probably just have to live with it - and, I dare say, more broken nights.

The house is full of lovely spring flowers in huge quantities which I bought today - daffies, tulips, irises, tiger lilies - and I told Roy about them and got him to feel the vase we bought in Amsterdam and the daffies in it. He seemed pleased. I bought a cheap leg of lamb today (£5) and told him I was going to cook Sunday dinner (as it were) for us both.(I said I'd set and serve two places and imagine he was sitting with me - and eat his as well like a child and an imaginary friend.) This seemed to please him as well.

Yesterday, when I brought in the bell, he said, in a kind of affectionate disbelief and gratitude, 'Oh, Bruce!'

The horizons of the world are shrinking to a very small compass - my mind is full of Roy, the sickroom, the routines, and, hovering in the background is the fear of this going on for ages - putting my immediate future in some kind of chaos (work? time off? house?). I've thought about having to give this up and have a nurse or find a bed somewhere for him. I think I shall have to ask for help if it goes on beyond Tuesday or so.

He's still turning himself, lifting his bottom without help, still psychologically quite vigorous - still smiles, makes cheeky remarks. Seems generally comfortable - the great cravings for oral lubrication - at least we can satisfy that - though whether we should be offering such a variety is an open question!

22 March Sunday 6:15pm: Although it is only a couple of hours ago, I'm not sure if I can project myself back into the helpless, weary, panicky state I was in for the first two thirds of the day.

I went to bed last night at 1:30am, having watched, and enjoyed Moon and Son - got quietly into bed, within two minutes Roy was asking for a drink. I can't remember what else he needed, but I put my head down at 2:30am. 5am he woke and was wanting drink? Pee? I can't remember - was that the awful, panicky session with him on the edge of the bed falling backwards if unsupported - me frantically trying to get his knickers off to let him have a pee? (How do you take the knickers off someone who's sat up and whom you can't possibly face lying down and lifting up again?) It was awful - him agitated, distressed - me feeling weak and agitated and distressed. That episode could have been at 10 o'clock when he next woke and I got up. I was feeling bewildered and disoriented.

Drawing up his injections - this all seems like days ago - it was this morning - the front doorbell rang. Not expecting anyone - ignored it. Eventually saw that it was volunteer Dennis - at 10:30 instead of expected 3pm. Then district nurse arrived at the door - I was very unwelcoming, I think. Dennis went off to get Sunday paper for me. He returned and went - I thanking him for the paper - then heard answer-machine message from volunteer co-ordinator saying that Dennis was coming. Continued with injections, then set about cooking leg of lamb, parsnips, Yorkshire pud and excellent gravy. Beautiful meat!

In the morning I'd phoned the community care team and asked to talk with Rob - I knew I needed help - bewildered, increasingly exhausted, I couldn't face any more. Before he came I decided we needed a nurse tonight.

I sat on the sofa - my head in a whirl - indifferently reading the paper, dreading a call from upstairs, hoping, each time I went up, that he was asleep (he slept long this afternoon).

Rob came and the cloud started to thin - the 'wilderness' (to use the imagery I chose) seemed no longer to be inevitable and for ever.

We talked about permission to die - Roy had said last night, 'I wish I wasn't here' - and I checked that back with him today: 'Well, things aren't excellent,' he said.

I made sense of the last week by saying to Rob perhaps we'd been too ambitious together in fighting on - perhaps we'd gone on longer than was natural or right - strayed from the path by the river of truth/integrity/right doing - into this wilderness - where we had been lost, alone, struggling - me resisting leaving him there just so I could get out. As we talked, I had a very clear mental image (vision?) of the edge of the wilderness which we were approaching (was it an aerial shot?), a long stretch of open scrub or desert and in the distance a town or city with a bright light shining from it. Just a momentary glimpse.

Rob was full of wonderful mystic/theological wisdom - talked of wilderness being a place you go to search for truth; a place you go to find reality; a place where you escape - and , of course, a place where you get lost.

I recognised how trapped I had felt - Rob brought fresh air into a stifling cell (a strange contrast to the wilderness image) - and that these last three/four days seem to have had a vastly extended timescale - it was only Tuesday I was at work - only four and a half days here in what was becoming chaos - my life having no more structure, no more distinction between night and day than Roy's.

Rob talked to Roy. Yes, he had had enough, but how did you do it? he asked. Rob evidently talked about letting go, about thinking of a holiday brochure - look at the pictures - where do you want to go - heaven? - perhaps - a tropical beach? - friends, no pain, good things. He told Roy that we must start saying our goodbyes - tomorrow. Oh gosh.

I spoke of the feeling that perhaps Roy and I had distorted the natural flow of things - that I had responded to his helplessness in such a way that it provided a kind of compensatory source of energy - and therefore he could carry on - that there was a symbiosis strengthening him and weakening me, postponing the natural point of departure, at the natural point of balance - but we could never have suspected or discovered this without doing it.

'Giving him permission' - assisting in his death, abandoning him, letting go, wow! - easy enough to theorise about - can I do it? Am I ready? Is it right? And it's not abandoning him.

I so much don't want us to say goodbye at a time when he may feel it's because I'm tired and played out - but Rob said that you can't isolate one from the other - that I am part of his death - he part of my life - that what's happening between us is part of a single, unitary process.

I don't want him to die: I have to face that, whatever preparations we have made - it's too huge a cataclysm for me - I look at him, lying in bed, his vacant eyes looking (to me) so tragic in their uselessness, his soft repetition of 'please' every time he's offered a drink; that lovely, familiar face, still alive, full of meaning, full of Roy. While exhausted by the demands, I still want him - without his illness - and without his frailty, his dependence.

And that's another strange thing (I may have noted it before) - his utter, naked, vulnerability and his acceptance of it. (As we went to sleep last night, he said: 'I rely on you a hundred...hundreds of millions percent.' I felt this could have been, 'Don't give up, don't let me down now,' - Rob felt it might be just affirmation. I was in no state to interpret such subtleties, but I think Rob was right.)

How different dying is from all one imagines - how long could he actually continue in this state? How long should he continue? Should we aid and abet the event? I actually don't know - we're not even talking about pharmacology; this is something much less tangible, but evidently equally as potent as drugs.

My call to the community care team this morning, I said, was about quality of his life and of mine. So it is. Neither of us has it now - so the key is removing Roy's absence of quality and returning quality to me through his death. Dear me. But we are talking, I suppose, about reconciliation with the inevitable - he is dying, I am alive (for however unpredictable a span!) - we cannot alter that.

I feel a great weight lifted from me - I am still tired, but not disabled. Rob's intervention provided all I had hoped for in terms of clarity, purpose, order - though there's still so much which is unclear and in disorder! Momentous times.

23 March Monday 11:30pm: I found it quite hard to hand over to the agency nurse last night and continued clucking about like a mother hen for some time - Roy insisted on opening his bowels before I went to bed, so we did that in private and I got the nurse in to help clear up. He peed simultaneously, but fortunately he was well padded up (pads lying on him) and all was absorbed - no soiled sheets. (He's always asked for a bottle previously.)

Feeling quite peculiar, lost, I bedded down in the spare room on my own - desultorily watched a little of Dr Strangelove (reluctant to abandon my freedom!) - took two sleeping tablets and a large whisky (as prescribed) and soon fell into deep, eight hour sleep. Felt much better this morning, went through morning routines (injections, drinks) with nurse present and did odd bits of business (brochures and things for work) before district nurse arrived for wash, nail clipping and general, quiet attention.

I've got a pile of bills paid now and oddments sorted out, including the latest drug order. District nurse and GP called in this afternoon - told them about Rob and our talk. They were kind and attentive (what GP ever visited so much when there's nothing for her to do except sign the prescriptions?)

Today, Roy has been moving more inwards, I think, much more of the detached chat - oddities (he woke up with pins and needles in his right leg; I was massaging it and he said something like, 'Do it like a cake' - at one point when he was just going off to sleep after drinks, he said, 'When are we going? I thought you were taking me to a wine-tasting.')

We started the 'letting go' conversation, twice, gently today. I asked him how he felt about things, whether he'd had enough. 'It's a struggle,' he said and indicated that there wasn't much pleasure left. 'Are you ready to go?' I asked. 'I think so.' 'It will be somewhere where there's no pain and struggle,' I added. He drifted off intermittently and chat was brought to an end by the front doorbell ringing.

He seems very peaceful - though there's evidence of lots of random thoughts surfacing - but now he doesn't distinguish their internal nature and is muddling them up with what is actually happening outside. During chat about the variety of drink he wanted he started talking about a fruit bowl (oranges included - he was having orange juice) and made the shape of round fruit with his hands.

Time has taken on a new quality for me - extended, tenuous - I find myself moving at a slow pace - sitting contemplating a document or simply sitting from time to time - unable to move myself along - though I've also done plenty (bills, papers, etc.; made potato salad to have with the cold lamb; went shopping, and so on).

I've written to the bank manager asking him about establishing the Roy Deakin Memorial Fund. I think it's a good idea - it will be a strong gesture of continuity for Roy and all his strength - along with the benefits (however small) for others in his position. (I think I'd want it to be to provide the smaller things which offer that extra quality - a last holiday - flowers, equipment, and so on.) Something to continue him. Needs thinking about.

I fell asleep on the sofa today after supper - and realised just how tired I still was. It will take some recovering from, I think.

Suggested to Roy that we might phone his mum - but he was never in much of a state to do so. He's not sat up on the edge of the bed today, and has been sleeping much longer and more deeply, I think. Wash this morning probably was exhausting, but I don't think that's all.

He still says hello to people who go into his room (district nurse, GP, volunteer, nurse last night) still positive about being civil - but, I think, there's less energy in it.

Talked to funeral directors today - no problems - but they won't embalm an HIV patient - so problems about having him home and certainly no chance (I imagine) of open coffin at the service. I've also been writing the stuff for the service booklet. I felt compelled to do it - not least because I shall be too overcome at the time, I think.

24 March Tuesday 2am: Went up at 12ish - just sat down again with cup of tea. What takes such time?
- Changed syringe driver and gave night injections
- He wanted water
- Had retching fit, and some vomit
- Wanted up on edge of bed
- More retching
- Him very shaky and distressed
- More water (expedition for ice)
- Glass too heavy, fetch plastic cup - OK
- Needed loo

- Lifted for commode, him very panicky and
  breathless and pale, I thought he was going to
  pass out
- Bowel movement OK
- Few minutes to be certain
- Then pee
- Bottle
- Wait
- Wait
- Good pee
- Cleaned up
- More drink
- Lifted back to bed
- Breathless
- Lay down
- Arm trapped, relieved, cream on bum
- Pad on
- Roll on back
- Knickers on
- Said he needed commode/loo
- Sure?
- No, can wait
- More water to drink
- Clean up pan, take out bowl, empty bottle
- Decide to increase diamorphine to 1gm
- He agrees
- Done, tea, write
- 2am!

He said to me, 'Are you alright?' - out of the depth of
his suffering, still time to be concerned for me.

24 March Tuesday: Last night - he had cold milk: 'It's so beautiful!'

Today he says: 'Yes it's time to go - but I'm still fighting.'

26 March Thursday 7pm: Today we passed a significant hurdle - my becoming quite clear that were Roy coherent he would not wish what was happening to him now to be happening - we've passed the point of no quality and last night I thought we'd entered negative quality without prospect of relief - discomfort, harassment, what little control we had has slipped away.

Yesterday (Wednesday) morning he was much troubled by endless coughing/gagging to clear his throat, and I felt it was really distressing him. More Midozolam suggested and given, followed by quiescent day with things getting more troublesome as evening came. I was on my own and hoped to spend a comfy night with him - after more Midozolam. Poor boy coughed and choked all night and gave no sign of realising I was there at all, spending the night with him.

(There's been - still is - a cat screeching and wailing outside in the weirdest fashion.)

Today, for the first time, he peed in the bed without warning - huge wet patch. Didn't like all efforts of district nurse to clear up, joint efforts to remake bed, suffered much in groin cleaning - obviously very painful. It was all done eventually - two hours or more - and district nurse went off to town - to be summoned back by registrar who'd brought urine catheter gear. When they

Top Broderip Ward, Middlesex Hospital, with Nurse John
Left A chilly expedition to Brighton, with wheelchair
Middle Our last Christmas together (1991). Roy's face is showing the bloating
effects of steroids
Right A seriously bad patch not long after the world trip (autumn 1991)

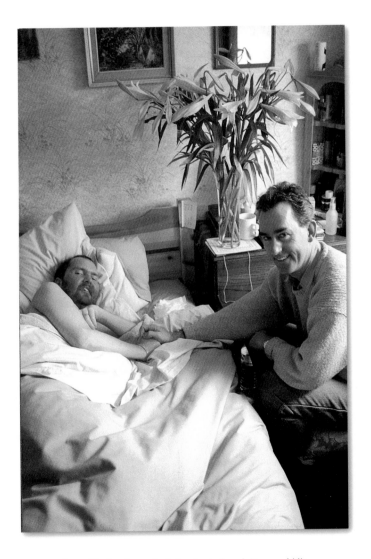

Almost blind, a few weeks before he died, with Terry and lillies went up Roy had been sick, but nurse removed big plug of gunge from his throat which - blissfully - eased the coughing. They put the catheter in and we changed the bed again. More Midozolam - Roy quite out of it. Suddenly, a calm, level plain: everything peaceful, clean and in order.

I had talked with registrar - 'I'm sure we're now past the point...' and showed her the living will document we'd both signed. Not that I felt that there were any practical consequences - I just wanted her to know. What did I want her to do? Nothing, I said, but don't do anything to keep him going. She felt nothing was being done 'officiously' prolonging life (intravenous feeding would have been, for example). She felt Roy had had enough - and that his body was at last giving out on him anyway

During last night Roy had said (in dopey, inward state): 'Going home' - which I thought might have meant the end. I'd said all the things to him before we went to bed - how much I loved him, that he was the best looking guy in the world, that he'd made me very happy. He thanked me in his lovely, diffident way.

Last night Nicky was here and very kind, thoughtful and supportive. First time she went up he didn't react, second time I called her up when I was with him - he recognised her, asked how she was and, as she left the room, waved his hand. He was still waving after she'd left the room. I came down and we cried in each other's arms for a good while.

I'm crying now at the thought of him - such helplessness, such open goodness and affection - it's so easy to overlook all that in the succession of bedpans, equipment, drugs and so on. There is so little time in the day to think. I haven't dared let myself feel half of what's been going on - how could it be borne?

I've just been sitting with him for a bit - turned him too. He's available enough to say he wants to be on his back or his side - and earlier while I chatted a little, I said I hoped everything was alright and he, breathed, 'Yeh,' and squeezed my hand. He's still there OK!

Yesterday (Wednesday) I spent most of the day trying to get text sorted out for the funeral - after myriad interruptions faxed off to designer at 10pm or so. He replied with first ideas this morning.

Volunteer Dennis stayed Tuesday night - I had blissful eight hours and felt strong enough yesterday to have night alone with Roy. Nurse coming in tonight.

It's been a wearisome nightmare in many ways - days and nights merging.

27 March Friday 5:40am: He died twenty minutes ago. Nurse woke me - breathing regular, but short and shallow. I asked her to leave us alone. No words - breathing gradually stopped. I said goodbye.

I feel very calm. He looks peaceful. It was time. Dawn is breaking. The birds are singing.

He knew it was time. He did it right. We'd said all we had to.

That's it.

5pm: Now they've taken him away and I feel simply that it has been accomplished.

27 March 1992: Vera sits with him a few hours after he died

The setting for the funeral at the Lighthouse

I sat and held his hand and cried a little - his delicate, expressive fingers - but felt quite detached from the body - it was, and yet hugely was not him. He looked peaceful - trials over.

I pottered around after the nurse left (she was quiet, attentive - lovely) then Rob came - a little tearful - paperwork - death certificate - and then the house to ourselves. I tidied up, did this and that, lit a candle by his bed and collected blue hyacinth and other flowers from the garden to put by him. Made arrangements with helpful funeral directors.

I felt, I suppose, affectionately aware of this now alien object in the bed - thought a little of all he had done and we had done - all that depended on his living energy - felt no great drama in death itself, nor in my reaction (not yet?) - there was a degree of peace, harmony in it all - fitness.

The family arrived (sister, bother-in-law, mum) - very simple, easy time. Vera thanked me for all I'd done for him - requested photos of her sitting by him, which I took. Ambulance arrived to take him to hospital for the post-mortem (Hospital for Tropical Diseases!) - I had a last moment, alone with him. Then they wrapped him up and took him away.

The DIARY

Part V

April - September 1992

It's Sunday 29 March: (two days after his death) playing Neil Sedaka - looking at our huge collection of photos. I cried a good deal today - feeling how the music reflects his wonderful lightness of spirit and how he taught me that the best of popular music expresses real and beautiful things. Rosie just phoned; she was very despondent - her mother's recent death, now Roy's. I said we shouldn't feel despondent about Roy - his life and how he'd dealt with AIDS was a triumph - that for months every day was a bonus, a gift - and for so much of that period we had had real quality time together.

Terry came over yesterday (Saturday) to discuss the funeral. Played the Anvil Chorus - that slayed me - how truly it exemplifies his energy - his sparkle.

Sue came over tonight. I realised how long it was since Roy and I had had a binge together. She had a few photographs of Roy at her place - wonderfully made up - frock, hat - looking radiant! It was a part of his life I couldn't fully share or fulfil - but she and Rosie liberated him - what a character - and, as Sue remarked - so hugely, obviously, deliciously masculine! 'Darling, there will never be another!' he sings.

On Friday (the day he died), Peter and Geraldine suggested we met in town. We went to the Covent Garden Wine Bar and the Café des Amis du Vin where the four of us had been together on several occasions - lots of champagne, splendid meal - completely rat-arsed again - and all evening talking about Roy. It was perfect, just what I needed - no reservations or self-consciousness.

There's been plenty of opportunity for talking about him - dozens of phone calls - at one point I felt I'd had more than enough talking. So many phone calls - kindly, loving, supportive friends. Today Vera phoned to see how I was - I was very touched.

Spent yesterday and today intermittently sorting papers, chucking out lots, felt improper going through his wallet - taking cash out, sending staff travel pass back - all very odd. I've been quite busy - partly because I've felt compelled to do things - but also periods of quiet, several bouts of weeping - especially (again) Anvil Chorus - he loved it so!

I've had brief moments of doubt and guilt - did I really treasure him as he deserved, did I really do all it was possible to do - did he really have the best possible deal we could offer?

I think so - friends have been saying how well we both did - there's admiration and appreciation - it's reassuring. Thank goodness we said all we could - I told him how wonderful I thought him, how much I loved him - many times. I think my cool slipped only slightly once or twice when I was on my beam ends - but not much.

I was curiously spooked last night after Moon and Son (a normally entertaining comedy about mother and son who dabble in astrology and spiritualism) - but went to sleep in our bed and slept well. The scent of blue hyacinths still fills the room - the smell of death for ever!

It's amazing how much there is to do! I've been washing constantly since Friday - everything nearly done now, I think. So much paperwork!

I'm not sure how much the estate is worth, but I think there will be enough to make life that little bit easier and to compensate for the loss of his income - we had no problem living up to our joint earnings!

There's the curious detail of our wardrobes - largely interchangeable - shall I wear any of his stuff? It will feel very strange.

On Friday night I felt enriched and strengthened by his death - somehow strong and confident rather than bereft and empty. It's been very strange in the house, though. Eerily empty, silent - especially after the thronging crowd that's been around recently!

I felt deprived of someone to do something for - after weeks of longing for relief it was awful to have no demands to meet - nothing whatsoever that I had to do for someone else.

I simply can't believe he's gone - there's that smile on the QE2 photograph - how can such energy, such spirit, just go? Of course it's commonplace!

Am I starting to idealise him? I don't think so. He was wonderful! I must eat.

4 April Saturday: Managed four days back at work this week, and just about got into the rhythm of things again.

I still can't believe he's not here - where's all that energy, humour, zest gone? After all the demands - and my longing for relief - I now long for him to look after again.

I'm uneasy out of the house for a moment longer than necessary - and rush back - to? of course, nothing. I feel like a parent must when responding to a baby's cry - it's as deep, conditioned, automatic now it seems. And I miss it!

I felt listless and physically depressed early in the week - and found it very difficult to work through the day - Tuesday I came home around 3pm, washed out.

Wednesday evening, my old friend David came round en route for Canterbury - it felt good - almost like a minor resumption of normal life - I bodged up a meal for him - but good to have someone to do something for.

I've just finished sorting out the pharmacy (well, half finished) and started going through Roy's things in his room - had very curious effect - removing the mystery? Taking away the depth of perspective another person owns? - there wasn't anything peculiar or revealing - but it was his territory - and only he knew it all, as master of the darker corners - now I've invaded, sorted, chucked out - I felt as though I'd chucked him out as well. Quite disturbing. On the other hand, he's not here any more, and nothing I do or don't do will change that.

Dozens and dozens of phone calls, cards and letters this week - great outpouring of affection and fond memories. Edith (our dear cleaning lady) let herself in and brought flowers - 'Roy - dear friend. Bon voyage,' the card said. It made me cry.

It's been very busy - sorting out the funeral and so on. Everything is in place, I think, spent time with Terry at the Lighthouse today; visited Lighthouse yesterday - met the wonderful caterer Billie Harris. The Lighthouse is a very special place - beautifully appointed, friendly, reassuring. I'm very tired again.

6 April Monday - Roy's funeral: The funeral was an extraordinary occasion - 'turning tragedy into triumph' as one dear friend described it - and it had a startling and radical impact on me and many of the people there.

During the last week of his life I had been preparing for the funeral, investigating caterers, the availability of the Ian McKellen Hall at the London Lighthouse, searching for a white suit to wear which had somehow grabbed my brain, talking to funeral directors, writing and arranging the printing of the funeral invitation and a memorial booklet, with curious intrusions of feelings of disloyalty to him while he was still living and breathing.

He had discussed his funeral with our dear friend Terry the previous autumn, and it had always been our intention that the event should be a party. I knew in my head exactly how I wanted it arranged, and never really considered the extraordinary risk of getting the whole tone and character of such an event wrong.

The event was billed as 'a celebration of his life and courage' and friends were invited to arrive an hour before the non-religious ceremony was to take place. They were greeted by a splendid array of beautiful food and as much bucks fizz or straight champagne as they could consume.

The chairs in the room were arranged in a U-shape with the coffin standing in the midst of the open end. Beyond the coffin a large colour photograph of him with his black rabbit was hung, flanked by the most spectacular and flamboyant floral displays, arranged by a florist friend of Terry's. Along the side of the room were hung several collages, each of twenty or thirty photographs covering his life from childhood to recent times. Cheerful music was played by two or three friends on the grand piano as we drank and talked and leant on the coffin with our champagne.

For the ceremony itself - which lasted far longer than we had expected - nearly an hour and a half - Terry found a most moving secular voice of reverence and love, interspersed with lightness and humour. He provided a strong and purposeful framework for the reminiscences of family and friends and the music which Roy had chosen. There were quiet, serious moments; many tears - and much genuine, joyful laughter. Rob, our counsellor consultant spoke, and in his few moments encapsulated much of his wisdom which had so profoundly influenced the quality of our lives. He spoke of Roy as a 'changeable man' - able to adapt with fluidity and courage to ever-changing realities. He spoke of the peace and reconciliation which he had found in the house.

The coffin was carried out to 'The Best of Times is Now' from La Cage Aux Folles - chosen by Roy and absolutely endorsed by me as the final word on his life. His mum and one or two of the family went off to the crematorium. I felt no urge to be present at what was, I felt, simply a utilitarian necessity - I had said goodbye to him and he had left long before - what remained in the coffin was simply a symbol, albeit a mighty one.

The sixty or so of the rest of us remained in the room and resumed eating and drinking for another couple of hours, weeping and laughing and talking and reminiscing - and getting increasingly drunk.

For me, the day was one of the rare occasions in my life when I felt I made almost no conscious decisions at all - I was swept up in a flow of events, feelings, relationships which had a momentum of their own. There must have been, I think, some kind of inevitability in the pattern and character of the day - an inevitability based on such long reflection and planning about the quality of the event and the people, and on the universal love and admiration for Roy - that once it was set in motion no more thinking or conscious decisions were necessary.

There was a remarkable variety of people present: Roy's dear mum, sister and her family and other relatives and friends from Yorkshire; my dear father (my mother chickened out at the last minute to my resigned disgust) and brother and sister-in-law; friends of Roy's and mine from all times of our lives and all parts of the country; a couple of my customers who were old, dear friends; doctors and nurses from the hospital and the community team; some of Roy's colleagues from work - such a gathering!

The community of feeling among everyone, many of whom had not met before - of love, of grief, of joy, of friendship - was such that it wove the hours we were together into a harmonious and transforming process - a catharsis which did take us through tragedy to quiet triumph.

Years after, friends have spoken of the impact of the occasion on their lives, on their thoughts about life and death, on their wishes for their own funerals and those of their loved ones.

7 April Tuesday: Yesterday went wonderfully - while the buzz of preparation protected me to some extent from the sorrow of it - listening to his music, making the tapes made me cry and reading my funeral piece to Terry choked me up. (It was hard on the day, too, though I got through it.)

Mary from Sheffield phoned in the evening after the funeral and asked how it had been - 'Wonderful!' I said - she sounded shocked, but it was true. There were laughter and tears - drunkenness (largely restrained) and so much goodwill, affection, warmth - vivid, loving memories of Roy from such a huge gathering of excellent people.

I felt very exhausted afterwards, but also content, fulfilled. I cried in the evening on my own in the kitchen over the cards and cheques (so many!) but steeled myself to start afresh today - the symbolic first day of a new life (some of it beckons - much of it seems unstimulating) which I've just got to get stuck into - the conflict is mainly that I just want to sit and think about Roy - everything else seems trivial, unexciting, flat.

I felt OK today and have sensed my old self and energies surfacing. On the tube home from work I felt very nourished, full - and realised (as it seemed) that yesterday had restored the complete Roy to me - memories of the suffering, weak, dependent, voracious patient gone, as the 'golden man' returned in full richness.

The funeral was entirely about the living man (well, yes, about our loss too) - but overwhelmingly about him from cradle to grave - got lots of glimpses, echoes, new insights from all kinds of people and angles. Relatives of his whom I hardly knew and whom I might well have thought felt that our lives were very peculiar told me warmly and without reservation how lucky he had been to meet me, to get out of the cocoon of Rotherham - to have had the chance to do so much. There was much appreciation, acceptance, of that kind - very positive, supportive and touching.

Though I knew the funeral was going on for a long time (much longer than planned) I had no sense of time during the ceremony - it was - well - luxurious. I did not want it to end.

I feel both that he's inside me and also that there's a staggering distance between us now - between now that is, this moment, and the smiling robust reality on the world trip and on the QE2 picture just on the desk here - was it a dream? No, of course, but how very far off it seems - how far off his reality here seems - though I feel his absence constantly - the empty house, the half portions of food, his barrel-bag still packed from the expedition to Yorkshire.

Just phoned David in Brighton - so pleased he came to the funeral but with the sad news of his lover being HIV positive. He's invited me to join a crowd of his friends for an AIDS charity concert that they've been organising next Sunday evening in Brighton. I had to take a deep breath before saying yes, but I must start to get out and about again, and this seems a peculiarly appropriate event. (David is one half of a cabaret drag act ('The Trollettes') which Roy loved. We used to follow them round the London circuit and I had persuaded David to visit us once on Roy's birthday as a surprise.)

Back to work on Monday - and the old kind of normality.

14 April Tuesday: I was going to say 'the urge to write has gone' - in once sense true (recording feelings) - but in other senses I've hardly stopped - endless letters - bills, post and (of course) work. Last evening I had two glasses of sherry and two glasses of claret and I felt slaughtered by 9pm - went to bed.

He's been dead over two weeks - I'm beginning to accommodate the fact, but still think of him constantly, miss him, miss the chat at home (how easily that's taken for granted, though I don't think that we did - but how important it is!) - miss him - planning, thinking about theatre trips - on my own? The sad, limited shopping expeditions (why when there are two of you do you buy stuff for six?!)

There have been some deeply touching letters - from Eric and Audrey about the funeral, from Ben and Tony with a huge cheque for Roy's fund - so sweet and fraternal; one from Roy's aunt saying the funeral was 'beautiful' - though she'd not known what to expect. Lots of cheques (nearly £1,300 to date) - one from the partners at Sue's legal firm - contributions from all over. The memorial fund seems to have touched people's hearts - several have remarked about not having thought about being ill and dying at home as an alternative to hospital.

The charity concert at Brighton (including Dora Bryan and all kinds of big names) was a splendid show - but I felt there was a real barrier between my rational perception of its excellence and my capacity to feel its pleasure and exhilaration. I felt Roy's absence so powerfully - he'd have loved it - even a Vicky Wood sketch!

I travelled home by train feeling curiously unsettled. David, Don, Del and all the (many!) others at the guest house and in the pubs were sweet and thoughtful, and I felt the power of their circle, their acquaintance with half of Brighton - home seemed very lonely and isolated from that perspective.

I was very busy on Saturday - went through most of Roy's clothes. Tried trousers on - chucked out a lot of his stuff and mine - bundled up for jumble sales. It all seemed fine - there were just one or two things which seemed to be essentially him - the lumberjack shirt and those dark blue, stretchy jeans (32" waist!) which I couldn't get rid of. Emptying pockets - anything which reached back to an action of his - seemed a bit strange - cutting the links. (Yesterday having the building society account put into my sole name struck me very forcibly - the white label obliterating his name for ever.) The envelope from Barclays today enclosing the requested new cheque book in my sole name was addressed to us both...

Interestingly enough, I haven't got round to sorting out the drugs and equipment for the community care team to take away. The gear is a pretty potent reminder, connection - even more than the clothes which he hasn't worn for such a long time. The 'pharmacy' has remained in a real mess - so much time spent in there - such responsibility - such duty - such life-enhancing stuff (how rotten I felt the once or twice I forgot a routine or was late - oh dear!)

I suppose the subconscious sifts through everything - there have been some odd emotions popping up - anger, guilt, jealousy (I think) over incidents long past - just twinges, glimpses which I've not dwelt on - they're real but of little account in the large picture.

I've wondered if I really looked after him as well as I could have done - was rough or thoughtless from time to time - only in retrospect does his long-term suffering (moment by moment) strike me - I was so immersed in the present, the actual, that perspectives didn't present themselves - it was all about comfort, reassurance NOW! I wonder how he managed the world trip - there was so much to endure for him - New York was a crunch - but we overcame it; he completely and voluntarily put aside whatever reservations there may have been deep down. He would not give up and (oh I do hope so) gained the rewards. Yes, there were extraordinary times - excellent times - I must re-read the diary to reassure me - yes, magic times - Barbados, flying fish, mountains - the sea - turtles - yes! Magic! - keep hold, Bruce!

The funeral was a grand finale - it left me feeling strong and comforted - proud of what we achieved - and true, I'm sure and everyone says - to Roy.

I postponed listening to the tape of the funeral till Friday night - fearing a devastating effect - but I found myself laughing and smiling as much as we had done on the day - the mere words seemed a little flat out of the dramatic context of the day - music, emotion, occasion, tears, so many people - but the words were good - far-reaching, rich, evocative of the whole spirit and life that were Roy's.

I have to resist being busy all the time - I find myself writing letters, doing this and that, filling the evenings - taking some little sleepy pleasure in TV, newspaper. (My sex drive has been active and satisfied on my own. It was diminished over the last months undoubtedly - often only getting relief when my balls ached with fullness - but it never went. I thought yesterday of the night Roy and I loved each other on our summer lawn in the dark - good times!) I think I feel less desperate to get back to the house than I did a few days ago, but the set of anxious feelings associated with leaving the house and going out - for so long I have been rushing back to it like a compass needle to north - and the sense of the vulnerability of it and its contents (especially mementos of Roy) and also a loss of self-confidence - can I manage on my own? Can I leave the house safe without his oversight? Can I cope socially? Shall I be OK on my own? Not dramatic, but definitely there.

I seem to be able to apply myself satisfactorily to work - I've had a very productive day today - and performed very well at the two training days in Bristol. I feel vigour returning - very slowly. Christina, our lovely GP, has given me some more Temazepan (at my request) - and it seems to be helping - though last night (went to bed at 9.30) woke up several times. All will be well, I'm sure, but I do miss him.

19 April Easter day: (Three weeks since he died) I've not cried since the evening of the funeral nor until now, I think, have I felt depressed. This has been brought on by reading the diary for 1989/90 and being reminded of Roy's suffering - his bewilderment, vulnerability.

Last night saw 'Hear My Song' with Peter and Geraldine - excellent, nourishing, witty entertainment followed by satisfactory meal at The Olive Tree - didn't feel his absence as strongly as at Brighton - able to let myself go more and enjoy the present.

When I'm not applying myself to some task at work, I think about him all the time - go to sleep looking at his picture on the funeral booklet.

I've been very busy - extraordinary degree of sorting out and chucking out - I'm not anxious to remove physical evidence of his presence (indeed chucking his stuff out is actually disturbing) but I seem compelled to get things in order - some things like his wallet I've not been able to dismantle, but I've been through practically everything else). I remind myself that the material objects (stuff that is junk or useless clothing, shoes that don't fit me) mean nothing - in clearing them out I'm not clearing him out - how could I? - there's so much else (internal and external) to remind me of him.

Yesterday I cut the hedges, tidied up the front garden, gave the lawn a rough cut (first of the season), tied the rambler rose back up. I've nearly sorted out the little bedroom and all the medical stuff. It's all something to do, I think, while I sort out how I'm to fill my life now - all this time. I feel again the desperate wish to get going with writing - what's the blockage to getting things published - what stops my stuff getting anywhere - what should I be writing and who should I send it to? When will I be fit to start again? When am I going to do something with the mountains of manuscripts in the filing cabinet?

I think his absence - permanently - is beginning to sink in. I'm tempted to fill the time with trivial household tasks - feeling them must be more important things to do - but what?

Money for the fund is coming along well - around £1,400 now - need to find ways of boosting it to generate real income - how long will the Charity Commissioners take to approve it? I think I'll go off and sort out the mailing list for it.

23 April Thursday: A really bad night after an entertaining and excessive evening with Ben in Earls Court - simply hardly sleeping and going over and over Roy's death - the minute by minute details - not threatening, unpleasant, but obsessive recounting, recording, reporting. I slept for a couple of hours until about 2am and then - physically uncomfortable, thirsty, mind full, hardly slept again - not till well after the dawn chorus. Also some very vivid dreams of strange inexplicable groups of good-natured people, not including Roy, with some warm, provocative sexy

interludes. Then I woke with an awful cramp in my leg. I was trying to let go of the endless replaying of the mental tape of Roy's last few minutes, trying patiently to get through it, then calm it down, saying to myself, 'OK old boy, OK,' trying to satisfy something, someone, letting it take its time and then trying to get to sleep.

I feel as though the natural mechanisms of sleep aren't working - is this because of the Temazepan? Or simply my exhausted, overwrought mind and body? There's certainly a real change - is it the tail end or the beginning of new patterns? It worries me. Shall I take any more? Will more tablets cause long-term problems? The pressure to sleep well is so great.

25 April Saturday: (Four weeks) What has struck me is the unpredictability of mood, feeling, memory, of energy levels, of the cycle of (brief) depression, sweet melancholy and bitter-sweet reminiscence. I feel a strange discontinuity from him - I look at the photographs and feel that they represent a world which doesn't belong to me any more - links severed, indeed, another world.

I find myself vaguely spooked from time to time. I haven't been able to finish watching 'Truly, Madly, Deeply' (which I started without any knowledge of its contents) for fear it will unbalance me - I've been aware of that inner world of chaos - of overactive imagination, of susceptibility to dark and disturbing images. In its simplest sense, I have been haunted by his death - a recurring picture - not distressing, just replaying the tape, as it were - though my main memories now are of times before serious illness - I wonder if I underestimated his pain - if I took sufficient account of it while he was alive - but also feel that such thoughts are a distraction - I did all I could, there is no cause for guilt.

This week I had to concentrate my mind on planning holidays - and thought again I might go to Barcelona and Seville, then this morning thought I might visit Lynn and Bob in Hong Kong. I phoned them and they seemed happy with the prospect. The autumn, perhaps. Lynn is in the UK in June and may come and stay. She said she wanted to see the video of our time in Hong Kong with them.

I'm beginning to get a sense of what I have to do - take initiatives, get on with planning, but it's a process full of conflict - today I thought about going to a film - phoning someone for companionship - but think I've decided I want to stay at home. Next weekend is a busy one - off to West Cumbria for training, Berwick for the retirement party, staying with friends in Maryport, so I'll clear the decks for being away (whatever that means - probably spending compensatory time here as much as anything else).

I spoke to community care nurse Vicky about the sleeping tablets - she was reassuring and said I should carry on - they are remarkable and I wake up feeling better - I just hope the need for them will diminish and natural sleep rhythms will return. Thursday was an awful reminder of the hours of sleeplessness.

I spent some hours staring pretty vacantly at the TV - reasonably discriminatingly - turning off the crap - but I found it difficult to switch it off finally and get to bed. Apart from first class things (Have I Got News For You?) - watching is actually rather depressing, I think - and there's so much about death and disaster!

4 May Bank Holiday Monday: (Five weeks) I do miss him. It's a kind of generalised 'less than best' feeling; I miss the intimacy - all the chat about the day, about inconsequential things; I miss the person next to me. Over the last few days I've travelled hundreds of miles by train (Cumbria/Berwick) and there's this feeling of the empty seat beside me - waiting for him to come back. I'm playing Elkie Brooks now (one of his favourites) - Pearl's a Singer - which has accelerated a sense of melancholy, of irreplaceable companionship.

I've been doing quite well - busy at work and at home, keeping everything in order as he taught me! It's been exciting to discover there'll actually be quite a lot of money in the estate. I think I shall pay a substantial chunk off the mortgage and probably do something to the house.

I've become slightly obsessed with getting things done to the house - especially the bathroom and waiting to see what the chaps' estimates look like - may include big wardrobe in my bedroom, cupboards in the study, kitchen, possibly small bedroom. Thought about loft conversion - but that can wait! There should be some cash left after most of that so I think it's probably the building society or something - it'll be nice having that sort of cash available.

If I pay off the Company share bank loan; smaller mortgage, possible pension, there should be lots more cash around each month. I'll need to be careful so as not to spend, spend, spend and leave no safety net for the future.

The actual reality of his day to day presence is fading - it's becoming the sheer fact of his absence which hurts - no one to phone up from hotels in far places - no one at home, interested in my movements, knowing when I'm due home - and except for the cleaning and ironing which dear Edith does - nothing new, surprising, delightful when I come home.

I'm having some difficulty with his ashes - not keen to have them hanging around the house; also a bit anxious about the photos Vera asked me to take after he died - will they be upsetting? I'll soon know.

He looks so well in this QE2 photograph - so full of life and his lovely good will. 'I'm so happy I could cry,' he said as we set off on the Orient Express. Precious memory of precious times.

I've just re-read the first article I did for Gay Times after the initial diagnosis - and filled my eyes with tears.

I can feel how easy it would be to try to fill the void he's left with someone else - but how fatal that would be. I feel very promiscuous in a theoretical kind of way - looking at men - searching for that magical being who'll light up my life - but of course, doing nothing at all about it - it would be dreadful! (It would simply be filling the void, and I couldn't face getting involved - all that pressure, energy etc.) I need to disentangle myself - and I think exploit my free energy - writing, work - being myself before thinking about partnership. I now know that partnership takes energy - and it is one of at least two choices - now there is more time and energy for other - different things. If I've always talked about doing things consecutively, then now I must return to finding out who I am and achieving the writing and other ambitions that haven't got anywhere so far.

I just watched some of the world trip video - surprisingly cool reaction - happy memories but manageable. Am I cutting all the pain off?

I must get somewhere - the theme of my diaries for twenty years - perhaps now, through the current success of the business I will get somewhere - again (like Probation) getting onto the national scene - this time, perhaps stay there and get further?

I feel listless and useless tonight. Perhaps just a little depressed?

17 May Sunday: It's not been as difficult or as painful as I expected. I feel alone, melancholy, sad, at a loss from time to time (and had one acute attack of loneliness in Bristol ten days ago), but I don't feel empty - I feel solid and ready to go forward. I miss him most of the time - all the time, I think - and look at the flourishing garden, the ears of oats and the dried flower arrangements, details he created - everywhere in the house - things that were expressions of his domestic happiness - how he is interwoven into everything, the physical fabric of the house.

I was anxious about getting the photographs of him and Vera at the deathbed and about the delivery of his ashes - but both were OK - I've not been dwelling on them. It's still intellectually difficult to accept he's gone - the fact - the end of all that rich, complex, lovely being.

I discover he's left me the present of a pension - and more money in total than I had expected. I shall enjoy that! (By some astonishing coincidence, he died on the very last day of his employment with London Transport, though he did not know it. I had not troubled him with the papers about the termination of his employment on medical grounds, and he could have had no idea that dying when he did, within a few hours of the deadline, gave me a little monthly pension for the rest of my life. The paperwork had been completed weeks before, and I had completely forgotten about it.)

I've booked five nights in Amsterdam (Alan may join me) and am about to send out invitations for the 'summer breakfast party' in July - the first big return to 'normality' and the usual patterns of the house's hospitality.

31 May Sunday: (Ten weeks) That I felt so little inclined to write since Roy's death, is significant, I think - though what it means I'm not sure. Before, it was a record of him and us - a record of unique, disappearing times; the writing was a part of my relationship with him, with giving it that dimension of permanence which life itself could not give; the writing was a kind of therapy - a companion under so much pressure when, at full pressure, there had to be a safety valve.

While I've done well, I think, in recovering my energy, in restoring more or less normal sleep patterns, in crossing the known and hidden obstacles to being a single man again, I've also had periods of real loneliness; of disbelieving sadness, sweet melancholy; and a deeper sense of 'who am I now?', 'does life have any point on my own?', 'is anything worth doing on my own?' that will take a long time to overcome.

I've reached the point of acknowledging that I must construct a new life - and I've positively started doing it - lunches, dinners, plays, films, planning the new bathroom, booking the holiday. And yesterday, feeling a bit limp in the afternoon, I thought, 'You can't not do things because there's no one at the moment to do them with.' So I went out to a film - actually feeling quite confident - then on to a gay pub in town where I chatted to two or three people, was briefly picked up by a charming scrounger, went to the piano bar, Madam Jo Jo's and Heaven; cruised unashamedly; came home at four in the morning, had bacon and eggs and went to bed. (Felt pretty grim today - very prostrate time with Sunday papers and coffee!)

The question is the quality of each day - that adjustment is huge. I had a great evening with Ronnie last week - Italian meal on Goodge Street, Drill Hall (wonderful show); espresso in late night Soho, on to Heaven - all excellent - time flew, immersion, but the rest of the time what deep pleasures are to be taken without him - and without sharing them with him? What do the evenings and weekends hold without him? Answer: the time has to be filled with quality activities and relationships - but there's such a risk that they'll seem shallow, unsatisfying in comparison. Need to deal with that - by taking everything as it comes, being fully in the moment - not comparing, regretting the past, but living in the present. That's hard, because having lost so much that was amongst the best - much else seems inevitably less rich.

The trip to Amsterdam is going to be a real test. I was thinking today how I must use the time there creatively - museums, concerts, finding real richness - perhaps I could write (it just occurs to me - there's a real challenge!). Where I am at any given moment is where my heart and mind must be - not let them constantly linger at home (or with Roy) where they have been for so long.

I listen to his CDs - and think of him - my throat is aching as I write - so far had we gone together, so deeply and completely. I went to dinner with Roger and Jane (who'd bought our first house in Balham from us) - and there was even now so much of the house which showed Roy's hand at work - tiling, painted mantlepieces, garden (I remember him building the aviary there or perched precariously on top of the garden shed sweeping the autumn debris off it).

Every day or so there's letting go of things that he touched or had around him - I thought today about the support hand-rails we had put up in the loo and the bathroom for him - they'll soon be swept away as the new bathroom takes shape; bottles of lemonade, ginger beer -

the last bit of the ice cream soda he so much enjoyed that night - oddly potent legacies.

I still look at the great collection of photographs with a kind of incredulity - how can that lovely, full, complete person and body simply have gone? From vigour, energy to nothing - to the canister of grey ash in the wardrobe upstairs? (It just crosses my mind that perhaps I should open it up and confront it. I don't know.)

I don't feel very strongly motivated about anything, I think (I'm working hard at work, though) - I ought to be using all this 'free' time to achieve things - though I'm keeping the house in order, doing bits in the garden, shopping, letters, bills, planning the party and so on - reading the papers - at one level profoundly passive and unproductive.

I have a general kind of angst as the weekend finishes - it's quite irrational because tomorrow (for example) holds nothing dreadful (though the demands and challenges are substantial) - and there's nothing else at present which can make any serious demands on my loyalty or time - I'm not even getting stuck into the memorial fund administration (though I pay all the cheques in).

I suppose I must be patient. There's lots of grieving and healing still to do - though I wonder if I can perform as I did without the stimulus and comfort of him.

19 June Amsterdam: (Twelve weeks) Memories of Roy are very strong here - the train from Schipol, the *dagkaart* for buses and trams, the tram into town - Leidsestraat - Taverne de Pul, Thermos, even the bistro where Ian and I ate.

After an infuriating journey (my 13.20 flight cancelled, late departure of 15.30 flight thanks to the World's Favourite Airline...) Ian was waiting patiently in the hotel. We had an agreeable evening - meal, lots of talk (mostly very serious stuff about him and his girlfriend), beers in De Pul, and then I went off to Thermos - not very busy but agreeable, including an affectionate, mutually pleasing session in the dark.

Got back to the hotel about 3am, but woke up feeling a bit peculiar - not sure if it's physiological or psychological - the thought that there would be a lot going on inside me in this place provided a little relief - perhaps there's some quite strong sadness at his absence - this was one of the particular places in which we had some wonderful times as well as some quite serious disagreements - not least about Thermos (the sauna), and though I certainly didn't feel anything but relaxed there - it did represent one part of me that (early on anyway) he wasn't entirely easy with. I can be the naughty boy now!

It poured with rain during the night - now bright and cloudy. It would be good if the sun shone!

26 June: Just back from the five days in Amsterdam - and missing him very acutely. I felt it beginning especially yesterday - almost all day just on my own - shopping, pottering, the Flower Market, wandering the streets, watching the people as we'd so often done together. Today, too, at the airport - so clearly remembering being there with him - spending our last guilders. The verve has definitely gone out of my continental shopping - much less joy in it!

First night (Thursday) went to Bistro de Vlier (with Ian) - where Roy and I went in 1990 - when he was beginning to feel weary and to lose his appetite. Then Sluizer restaurant (twice) - where he so loved the warm goat's cheese joke at the expense of my struggling Dutch (what I'd actually said seems to have been, 'I'd like the warm fuck,' which sent the entire staff into fits of merriment all evening). And to the Flower Market (I bought flowers for the room as usual) - well, everything full of memory - it has only crept up on me towards the end. (I bought our usual selection of duty-free perfumes for his sister and nieces - just as we'd always done - probably for the last time - letting go so much!) but I also had a great time - the sauna gave up its usual riches - steamy Greek in the Turkish bath; friendly Indonesian in a dark corner; lovely, brief horizontal lovemaking in the dark room; pleasant pickup by New York Indonesian Chemical Engineer on the last night - and so on.

Then there was the time with Ian and Katie, trying to help them through the crisis in their relationship. (While we were not holidaying together, I had suggested Ian might come over to Amsterdam to spend some time talking. A couple of days after he had arrived Katie came over for two days as well - lots of serious talk, some drama between them and their counsellor (including my storming out of the restaurant where we were having dinner - I was so fed up with his recalcitrant stupidity) but I think there was real progress and greater clarity for them both about where they were to go.)

A good time, though, and I was very happy to be there - to pig out gastronomically, sexually, sleeping long, etc - and have surely put back all those pounds I so carefully tried to lose beforehand!

But the house is empty, and he's gone.

19 July: (Four months) Had a quite lovely afternoon and evening yesterday at Kenwood with Derek, Ken, Andrew, Mark, Sally, Ken's mother - open air concert with pink sparkling wine, canapés, strawberries, fruit kebabs and fireworks at the end of the concert. Everyone came back here and talked and drank for an hour or two while Andrew and Mark stayed till about three.

The whole day was excellent - I felt comfortably part of a group - accepted, unreserved, easy. Everything was delightful. I also felt satisfied, even exhilarated by the party here on 28 June - the 'summer breakfast party' - about twenty eight people came - lots of people I was really pleased to see - including Roy's registrar and her ex-patriot hubby, Geoffrey.

Chris, the butler, was a great success and the tapas-style food which I'd cooked looked wonderful. Two dozen bottles of champagne lasted the day - and the last guests were trickling off by 11pm or so (twelve hours on the go!) and Dalziel and David stayed the night. It was wonderful having two such golden young people arrive unexpectedly - David enormously impressive in the morning stripped to the waist in his pyjamas - sexy, lovely to look at, quite at ease - gave me and the guests a real sense of the exotic. And Dalziel was lovely as always. Monday (last day of my hols) we had champagne breakfast in the garden, and David worked out on the lawn (Dalziel sat on him while he did press ups!) and then they hosed each other down - Dalziel stripped to the waist as well - until the builders started drifting out into the garden to start bathroom project.

There have been lots of good times - meal and Drill Hall with Ronnie and Canadian Greg - then Village and Bang where we stayed till 3.30am or so - felt weak and useless all Sunday!

Last fortnight saw the great step of my first masseur ever - in Bristol within easy walk of my regular hotel - a very pleasing, relaxing and satisfying encounter - friendly and uncomplicated: coffee, fag, massage then gentle finish. £40 is a bit much to do it often, but I shall certainly go back. I was pleased to discover it wasn't a problem for me, no guilt, disgust, reservation. I left walking on air.

Summer party on the ward at the Middlesex last Thursday, pleasant occasion - nice people - talked to Bill (Keith's partner) - we talked about our grieving - going through very similar feelings - and both, I think, doing very well. Last night (after the Kenwood concert) - while we had the furs and the stilettos out - I looked at Roy's picture on the wall - and thought he'd have approved. In logical terms why that should matter, I don't know, but it means something somewhere - though I don't think I'm going to be inhibited from doing things of which he would not approve.

Talking a lot with Andrew at Kenwood yesterday I felt very liberated, quite camp and witty - he seemed surprised/pleased as he'd seen me as 'reserved' before - but he also brought out a rather more persistently outrageous streak in me that I've experienced recently - I felt good, at ease, confident, whole - throughout the entire occasion.

I've not been feeling too well for a fortnight or so - heavy, nasal/chesty cold and my brain's been a bit addled - though I've managed to keep all functions alert and active - even when feeling grotty. Work is going well, though I'm dashing about all over the UK - very wearing, especially appalling BR reliability recently - and I feel half oppressed by the amount of demanding stuff which has to be done in the next six months. Oh for remuneration with less sweat!!

Had lunch with Jeremy H on Friday - very agreeable Italian meal in sunshine on the pavement - good vigorous conversation about real matters - he let me talk a good deal about Roy - and lots of good, real personal stuff. I wasn't keen to leave and to get to my next appointment.

There's so much in prospect - Drill Hall and a meal with Sue Lodge next weekend; dinner with Ken and day trip to Boulogne with Helly the following weekend; to Dan and Jude in the country the following weekend - and so on! When I'll get the hedge cut or world-beating TV scripts done I've no idea!

Went to 'Six Degrees of Separation' with Katie last weekend - splendid American play (about a young guy who pretends to be Sidney Poitier's son and exploits his hosts' gullibility) and had very agreeable after-show coffee and brandy. My first visit to the Royal Court - lots of firsts these days!

I just opened the bottom draw of the desk and found a notice of death card, funeral booklet - reflected on the oddity of getting all that stuff ready while he was still alive. There was obviously no doubt in my mind that the end was near and in fact the timing was exact.

10 August: (Four and a half months) I've been sad and a bit depressed this weekend. Looking through photos on Saturday (for the second Gay Times article and to give to Terry) I cried for a few moments, and I think grief has taken a slight grip - I did feel low when I went to bed. And this morning - I just noticed the little plastic box of black and white paper clips and desk miscellanea, map pins and other office odds and ends in the study which he'd bought me, and thought how no one has ever bought me such wonderful presents - chosen to give me particular, unique pleasure - no one has ever known the peculiarities of my taste so well (saucepans, Mapplethorpe calendar and cards, Liberty bow tie, candle lamps and so on).

Perhaps talking about him (and the world trip) with Dan and Jude yesterday and a little at Roy and Andy's party on Saturday has stirred things up (as well as news of the QE2's grounding off New York!) - I certainly feel moved and sad - not surprisingly perhaps (I was also copying the funeral tape).

Last weekend was very rich and busy - Friday evening dinner with Ken in Streatham - Derek, met Roy and Andy (neighbours down the road here) and Chris and Dave. Good evening, then trained from Streatham to Victoria and Canterbury for night with Helly before Saturday in Boulogne - champagne on the ferry for breakfast then bars and long lunch in sunny courtyard and too much food for us to finish!

Then Sunday afternoon Ben came to talk about his crisis (very useful, sad, companionable meeting followed by dinner here) then friend from Cumbria turns up to stay the night - and launch the new bathroom in spectacular style - what a very good night! I couldn't believe what a weekend of exhausting riches it was!

I've been feeling knackered generally - whizzing round Britain during the week (last week, for example, two days in Bristol, one in Derby, afternoon in Chichester). This morning - while I wait for London Electricity to come and the electrician checks out the new electrics - I do feel washed out - it may have something to do with alcohol - every evening for ages!

There's such a busy week ahead: two days in Bristol, two days in Lancashire (both training) - then Ronnie on Saturday and Audrey and Eric on Sunday. Should I calm down and sleep a bit?!

22 August: (Five months) Last week I booked the holiday in Thailand (my first time) - with some reservations, I think: is it the best way of recuperating/enjoying myself? Unusual for me to be uncertain - it's got something to do with travelling alone, I think. But I'm pleased!

I've been saying to people recently that Roy is 'becoming part of the past', rather than the present - I suppose I do feel that - but also feel saddened by the change - as he becomes part of the past, so I must face being alone - even more alone as memory, immediate, sharp, accurate memory fades - I feel a pang of sadness even as I write - there he is on the QE2 with me - just a year ago - what a year - just one year?

How remarkable a companionship it was - and the joy that it is not sentimental re-creation or nostalgic fictionalising - it was wonderful at the time - and we both knew and acknowledged that. How lucky, how lucky!

21 September: (Six months) It's the night before Thailand and I'm feeling tired, subdued, even a little depressed, I think. I performed splendidly at training in Keswick yesterday but feel very under the weather today - it may have been the midday sherry - and being woken at 8.30am by a client on the phone.

I'm hugely satisfied and excited at having made such progress with this manuscript - at last something real, solid, rich, achieved. I've been thinking so much about Roy as I wrote, as I travelled, he's been strongly with me - I don't quite understand how or why, but the time has been going through my consciousness regularly and calmly - I occasionally feel acutely sad - melancholy - listening to music or whatever, but not wretched. Life has been too full - frantic - for that or for loneliness.

I've travelled thousands of miles in the last two months by train, addressed hundreds of trainees, been to theatres, films, parties - there's so much to do, so many people to enjoy.

Thailand will be a transformation - I must rise to it physically and spiritually - refreshment, recuperation, meditation - feed the spirit and start a new life on my own!

Grief, Anger and Hope

October 1990

When I returned home from town today, knowing that he would have set off for the train north to see his mum, there was a scented rose of the purest salmon pink, picked from the garden on the kitchen table, with a note under it: 'Much love,' it said.

I am moved by this gift of tenderness - it is by me as I write - for, while thoughtful and affectionate, he is not typically demonstrative. Recent months have brought us closer, certainly, but this rose touches me deeply in its simple symbolism and beauty.

Knowledge of death sharpens the mind and the heart: its bitter reality leaping out of the dark with sudden drama. Lying in bed with him tight in my arms, I feel his warmth, the rhythm of his breathing, lay my hand on that loved, familiar forehead and suddenly am numbed with a vision of his absence - absence for ever (how precious is the flesh). Even now, when he is away from home I wander round the house, strangely helpless on my own. I pick up his familiar things and, for a moment, it is as if they no longer have an owner, are mere mementos of a former life.

But what, for me - I think guiltily - are these mere pinpricks of pain beside his great sorrow - his not knowing from day to day if he will feel ill or well, his uncertainty that he will see next Christmas, his grief and outrage that his once lively and co-operative body has been subverted, invaded, poisoned? Close though we are, I only glimpse the depth of that horror.

Yet, once the early days had passed - the days and nights of grief and anger and tears, when death itself appeared to hover behind him - since then he has been in generally great spirits - even in hospital sparkling and attentive - his old self which always prompted - and still prompts - such warm, affectionate responses from others. I marvel at his strength, his stability, the resources which must lie at the core of his being, now feeding and invigorating him.

There are dark hours for him, hours of lethargy and queasiness; there are restless nights made intolerable by torrential sweats and livid nightmares. There are moments of uncomprehending rage or deepest sadness when all that is unlikely to happen, when all that may be lost for ever snaps sharply into focus.

He is not now ill - an early touch of PCP seems to have been suppressed by pentamadine, and oral thrush is under control with antibiotics - yet his vital energy is ebbing: a few hours' exertion one day makes him almost incapable of getting out of bed the next, and he almost always falls quickly asleep with his head in my lap when we watch the television. Things are not as they were, not by a long way.

Over last Christmas and the New Year his persistent debility, night sweats and loss of appetite made him suspect something serious was wrong. The several weeks of painful sinus infection and dry convulsive coughing took him eventually to the doctor, fearing the worst. But that premonition did nothing to soften the steely impact of the positive result.

That day, I arrived home late in the evening (oh god, to be absent at such a time!) - to find him sitting pale, bolt-upright in bed with the news instantly, cataclysmically on his lips. Stunned, by turns we talked mechanically or wept in each other's arms - faced suddenly, unambiguously with the possible end of all we had built together, all we had planned for the future, the final act of a life that had hardly begun. That night there were moments of rage and grief, of beating the bedclothes with despair and frustration, but nothing to the climax of reaction ahead.

The next day (a Friday) we spent together at home, intensely, closely, talking - amongst much else - with uncanny coolness about very practical matters - about wills, life assurance, maintaining our income, paying the mortgage - talking as if he were about to die - for that was how it felt to him: it seemed as if the news had itself not only given him the disease, but also pronounced a sentence of imminent death.

In the height of the early shock, we agreed to tell no one else. This fearful, depressed reaction rapidly gave way, as we thought of our circle of kindly, supportive friends, to a determination to tell most of them: secrecy would only intensify our sadness and cut us off from those very resources which would provide comfort and hope.

It was the sense of injustice which, I think, he felt most - we had both for so many years been careful, responsible. It must have happened before he knew there were risks to take or choices to be made - eight, ten years ago: oh, the unfairness of it! 'Why me? Why me?'

The following evening (Saturday) he was booked to go out with two dear friends of ours (we have always enjoyed some social life independently of each other) while I remained at home. I spent much of the evening recording the week in our diary.

Very late, the three of them returned, our friends leading him pale, unsteady, drunk beyond measure from the taxi. He slumped on the stairs, weeping raspingly, while they went into the front room in floods of choking tears. Evidently he had told them. I closed the door and stayed on the stairs with him. He was desperate, furious, grief-stricken, violently, helplessly angry: 'Bastard life, bastard life!' he hissed again and again through his sobbing.

Slowly, the peak of anger passed. We returned to the room. Our friends' grief at the thought of losing someone they loved so much - and others who might fall victim too - was violent, and he and they cried and cried, hurt and fearful, as we sat successively in each other's arms till early morning, the tear ducts aching and wide open.

It was a time of the most extravagant grief I have ever been close to - dear people overcome, overtaken, utterly overpowered by one commanding emotion. I alone remained dry-eyed and unaccountably calm.

He and I woke together on Sunday strangely relaxed and cleansed - the depths seemed to have been plunged and were now passed. The climax - the nadir - was now over.

So we told many - most - of our friends during the following days and weeks. It prompted such an outpouring of love and support and concern that it was exhilarating and beautiful. It was as if knowledge of death allowed hearts to be opened in a way sometimes only apparent at funerals - when the frank declaration of love and appreciation is tragically too late to enrich the life of the loved one.

There is no cynicism in this - for even doing our best, most of us have, on occasion, learnt only too late that we could, should have done better - should not have wasted those precious times when love was felt but not shown.

If our friends comfort and sustain us, there is also much else that gives strength: we feel great pride and pleasure in our gay and lesbian brothers and sisters and in our community especially, now, knowing at first hand at a time of need their practical, effective and generous responses to the reality of the virus and disease; pride that 'our' people and their many friends have confronted the nightmare with imagination, responsibility and maturity.

Strength and comfort come too from the NHS doctors and nurses in clinic and hospital who have not simply provided efficient medical services, but have also demonstrated great goodwill, patience - and humour. None of us should expect less in any circumstances, but we are grateful to find such qualities in the midst of our crisis.

Knowledge of death concentrates the mind and the affections. We do not feel that we have wasted our nearly seven years together - we have had a full, varied and modestly adventurous life; we have not seriously abused or neglected each other; we have had a good time in two excellent homes with many, much-loved friends.

Now we know all that could end soon, we are changing our priorities to some extent: it is less relevant to save for the future now - we should spend and enjoy. We should do some of the things we've always wanted to do. We should make the most of the time, the people, the opportunities. We should do everything we can to stay in our home - if he must be ill, let it be here - and so I must earn to compensate for the possible loss of his wage. We must sort out our practical and financial affairs.

So-we have flown Concorde (ninety minutes of supersonic luxury, champagne all the way); next we may blow our savings on the Orient Express or on a flight round the world; we are spending more time with our friends; we are going to more concerts and plays; we are taking more quiet time together; I have left a modest, stable job and set up my own business; we have had a serious session with our solicitors and executors. Our house is in material order; we are not in retreat.

He still cries himself to sleep from time to time, fearful of the future; is still occasionally angry and resentful; is often weary. I sometimes wake up with tears in my eyes and an ache in my throat, or find myself about to weep on the street or the train. If I let myself, I fear the future horribly: his suffering, my inadequacy, the end, whenever, to come.

Our suffering does not compare with those who have been through to the end, or have lost their loved ones: we still have each other; he still has the strength to visit his mum in the north, and the spirit to leave me a sweet-smelling pink rose from our garden. If only it could last for ever!

* * * *

In the early days of knowing he was HIV+ (in March this year) we found it worrying and difficult to be out of each other's company for any length of time. For him it was, I think, his shocked sense of sudden weakness and vulnerability - alone, he felt at risk from the demon in his body, and frail in a world which had suddenly delivered such a hostile blow to his hopes. For us both it was a compelling need simply to be together, while my early, and continuing fear was that something dramatic might happen when I was away from him.

I have found it very difficult, without a sense of unreasonable guilt, to continue meeting the demands of my business, and to allow myself to become absorbed in the outside world and its concerns. It's a particularly painful process because I miss his best hours in the day: he's asleep (or at least sleepy) when I leave in the morning, and weary by the time I return in the evening. Yet it obviously has to be done if we are to stay here, comfortably in our home, when he can no longer earn.

After eight weeks or so we had just about come to some kind of terms with HIV on a day to day basis, though he was not in good health and we feared there was definitely something wrong. He continued to work throughout that time, taking his lunch hours for clinic visits, which we made together.

I arrived home one afternoon to find him packing a suitcase: he was to be admitted to hospital for investigation of a patch on his lung which had shown up on the X-ray.

It was devastating news. In dealing originally with the reality of the positive test, one of our strategies had been to reflect that at least the result did not make him ill, and that it could be a long time before illness emerged. That was swept away - he now had PCP, one of the most typical 'opportunistic' infections of a damaged immune system, and we had to accept that he was more vulnerable than we had hoped.

The shock was compensated for, to some extent, by there now being something more definite than the previous general sense of unspecific malaise and anxiety: now there was a focus for concern and a busy team of doctors and nurses, investigating, monitoring, advising and prescribing.

The week in hospital was extraordinary. The staff were remarkable in the quality of care they offered - changing his sheets, for example, two or three times a night after the worst sweats (a quality of care which had the reverse effect on my confidence, of course, in terms of what I felt I could provide for him at home); our friends turned up in their crowds, some of them staying around for hours. Much of the time he was in great form - the bright, affectionate, humorous chap we'd all known and loved over the years - he looked a picture of blooming health.

There were those in the ward who were very ill, and we were both reminded - he especially - of the great variety of ways in which the body can be invaded and wasted, and of the potentially helpless, lingering last stages. It is that, certainly, which he fears for himself, and I fear for us both.

It is almost uncanny, but I think we have both grieved already a good deal for his death - not accepted it, not resigned ourselves to it - but faced it as a real possibility, together mourned for it and begun to prepare for it. It is the most terrible truth - for him the theft of twenty, thirty, forty years which he (like us all) assumed lay ahead of him - half a lifetime of relationships, holidays, pleasures, adventures; for me, the loss not only of those anticipated years of enjoyment together, but also of my centre, my anchor in an uncertain and lonely world.

Let him have strength and health, but let him not linger helplessly and painfully.

In the early days, amidst the grief and the drama, we were also very businesslike in attending to practical affairs, and we have since been grateful for that foresight.

After a couple of years living together, we had made wills, appointing each other as executors along with his brother-in-law and my brother, and making each other principal beneficiaries of our estates.

Knowing, however, that our relationship had no status in law, and that meddling bureaucrats or unsympathetic medical authorities could stand between us or seek to discount our wishes (all facts and possibilities which make us angry and indignant) we wanted, in view of the new situation, to strengthen our position.

We arranged a meeting with or solicitors and executors. First, we signed slightly revised wills. Second, we read out, and then had signed and witnessed a statement declaring our absolute wishes with regard to our rights over each other. This says, essentially, that all persons and authorities are to regard each of us as nearest next of kin of the other with regard to all practical and financial matters, with regard to hospital visiting and access to medical information, and with regard to funeral arrangements. We also appended a paragraph from the 'Living Will' of the Voluntary Euthanasia Society which asks that life should not be artificially or painfully prolonged.

This declaration probably has no ultimate legal status, but it at least means that our solicitors and families are in no doubt at all about, and have formally (and willingly) consented to our wishes.

Finally, we each signed *Power of Enduring Attorney* for each other. This does have full legal status, and is enforceable in the courts. It empowers each of us to act in law *as if he were the other person* - to sign cheques, make contracts, dispose of property and so on. Within the current state of our unhelpful legal system it is the nearest a gay couple can approach to achieving the rights and benefits of marriage. It is the most absolute act of mutual commitment in legal terms.

To those who have not thought deeply about such matters, or who have not experienced the sheer indifference - brutality even - of families and people in positions of authority in the face of a gay partner or bereaved lover, all this may seem completely over the top. It is not: when it comes to the crunch our world can still be mean, hostile and cruel. The risks are too great to be left to chance.

So, when he was admitted to hospital, it was one less anxiety to know that we'd been through all the formalities - at the worst I could show an obstructive sister the Power of Attorney and threaten to go to court.

In the event, it was, happily on this occasion, entirely superfluous. Without exception the medics and nurses - several of them ingenuously gay - welcomed me as his lover without reservation. That itself was a healing experience for us both.

Friends and medics all ask if I have been tested. I have not been and have no intention of being as long as I am well. What would the knowledge achieve? It would be reassuring to know that I was negative, but knowing of a positive result would simply double our anxiety and stress at a time when we need all the strength and optimism we can muster. I am much more concerned about infecting him with my summer cold bug than I am about my HIV status: that is no risk to anyone.

Our friends' reactions have been a source of strength and comfort. Telling our parents seemed, in comparison, to be a thorny, dangerous path to walk.

He had never told his widowed mother that he was gay, and we were now confronted with delivering a double blow to her peace of mind. She had been anxious for some time about his health - worrying on the phone and in her letters - and we suspected that she might - in her worst moments - have lighted on the truth.

His admission to hospital meant we had to face the issue: she would be deeply hurt and offended to learn that she had been excluded, and we had no business to deprive her of her mother's rights.

On the second night of his admission, when she already knew that he was in hospital, I phoned her, with Roy's and the family's agreement, to tell her what I could, going as far as her reaction allowed.

I had carefully thought through what I should say and how she would react, and was ready to be frank.

We were on the phone for an hour. It was clearly appalling for her, but she showed the same strength and courage which has been so clear in his own reaction to the crisis.

'Just tell me it's not AIDS,' she said at one point, and I thought how a mother's heart misses nothing. 'He should never have left home,' she said; 'What's he doing messing about with blokes?' 'He should come home to be looked after.' So we talked slowly through it all - that staying at home or leaving would have made no difference; that it was not some isolated encounter, but that men had always been his choice; that his home, which he had built with such love, was here, with me.

And she heard it all, absorbed it, and sadly but toughly accepted it. Remarkable people, some mothers.

Since then she has stayed with us for a weekend with daughter and son-in-law, and she has been cheerful and supportive and undemanding.

So, now he is with her in the north for two or three days - and she won't ask him to clip the hedge or move the furniture as she used to. They will have time together for the first time since she has known the full story, and it may be an emotional visit. They have always been close in all but that one matter.

In his absence, I write this. It is partly my way of processing and understanding what is happening to us - even, perhaps, of keeping control of it through the discipline of analysis and the movement of the pen across the page. But there is also a wish to share our experience with others - to make a contribution to understanding and coping with this nightmare which haunts all our lives, and can pounce on any one of us at any time.

We've done nothing remarkable, suffered nothing exceptional. We've found our love sustaining us in the crisis and we're going to live actively and happily while we have time. We are proud of what we are and of what we have achieved together, and we have not wasted our opportunities.

And the pink rose he left for me gives off its fragrance, reminding me how much I love him.

The Best of Times is Now

January 1993

He died at home, in his sleep, just after five in the morning that Friday, three weeks ago. His breathing slowed, thinned and evaporated effortlessly. I held his hand and said goodbye. I did not cry then.

The previous ten days had been rough for both of us: for him as he became increasingly helpless - recently blind, progressively debilitated, unable to swallow more than a few drops of liquid at a time, subject to the tyranny of congested chest, nauseous stomach, and unpredictable bowels; for me, working and nursing, beyond all the boundaries of physical and emotional resources I had ever crossed before.

Yet though he had suffered so much, it was really only at some point on the last day that the final hair's breadth of quality of life disappeared for him - the point at which I knew, and I'm sure he knew that there could be nothing more to take pleasure in. Only then was he ready, and was I willing, at last to let go.

For two years, knowledge of the prospect of death had had its influence on every aspect of our lives: we had raged against the implacable reality of HIV, wept, grieved and speculated; we had put our affairs in order - wills, powers of attorney, planned the funeral; but, above all, decided that we were not going to waste a moment of the time or a drop of the energy we had left together.

As an increasing burden of illness undermined his strength and capacities, between long periods in hospital, he continued to work, we flew on Concorde, went to America, continued eating, drinking and spending time with friends whenever possible, and, in our grandest assertion, spent a month travelling round the world in some style (we didn't have the cash for the trip, so we borrowed against the security of his life assurance policies - a transaction which the bank, though willing, actually found more difficult to deal with than we did. We knew what we wanted and got on with it). There was no desperation, simply determination that the time we had left should be rich and memorable.

What mattered for us both was quality of life, not quantity. His choice for a shorter and better life was uncompromising and we were fortunate in having a medical team who understood such things and offered that choice. It's one of the mysteries of such things that in choosing quality we were also granted quantity - far more than anyone expected.

Such clarity about what we wanted in general and in particular - to be up and capable for this day, this visit, this weekend, this event, to be fit and equipped for a month round the world - made the medical team's task that much simpler: their planning - like our own - was directed to more or less immediate, specific goals: in the early days, they were all external, active events; as time passed, they were less to do with activity and more about achieving a comfortable state of being.

We learnt that quality of life is not necessarily some grand and sumptuous state, and absolutely not about hankering for some vision of what might be: it is about achieving the best that is possible in the present moment. While he was active and relatively well, quality was achieved by exploiting all our available resources - physical, emotional, financial - and doing everything that we could - Concorde, the world trip, and so on, so that we could never reflect regretfully, 'If only...'

As he became weaker, house-bound and eventually bed-ridden so the scope of quality narrowed, adjusted progressively to what was possible, but its richness did not diminish.

What he was able to do, with astonishingly courageous realism was to reconcile himself to each loss of strength, faculty, opportunity and to live fully within the boundaries of what was possible within the present. Two examples illustrate this extraordinary adaptability - the wisdom of which I could only follow with humility.

For the last six months he was - as we both wished - at home. In the early days he would be up and about for a few hours each day while I was out at work and then have an afternoon snooze. He got up when I came in, we ate together and spent the evening talking together, with friends, on the phone or watching TV or videos. Gradually he spent more and more time in bed during the day, getting up only after I'd been in for an hour or two, and spending just a couple of hours dozing in my lap on the sofa before going back to bed. They were hours of quiet, undemanding, lovely intimacy.

Exploring his perception of the quality of his life, the consultant asked him if his day with this couple of good hours was good enough. In a powerful phrase - all the more so for its being quite untypical in its language - he said, 'It is sufficient'. And he continued to enjoy those couple of hours until he could no longer haul himself up and down the stairs, when the criteria for quality had to be redefined once again.

The other indication of his capacity to hold precious the moment was much later when he was blind and bed-ridden, and when the arena of quality was becoming relatively microscopic. He was eating nothing and drinking very little - that little dripped into his mouth from a syringe. On two nights he woke up wanting a drink. The first time he asked for milk. I brought him half a pint straight from the fridge, and he insisted on sitting up on the edge of the bed. He drank half at one go and said, 'That is so beautiful.'

On the second occasion, after reviewing the range of drinks in the house, he said he'd like an ice cream soda with ice cream in it. He had one, adored it, and promptly asked for another - the evident, immediate pleasure being enriched by childhood memories of similar, exceptional indulgence.

In the midst of raging illness, debility, helplessness, such moments have a kind of glory about them - in spite of everything he was able to give himself over to intense pleasure.

There was, then, a hair's breadth of quality, which was, at that time for him, no less full and real than drinking champagne on the Orient Express had been the previous year. He could release the Orient Express as a possibility and savour the next focus of quality though it was on an ever-diminishing scale. Only when there was nothing left on the scale did he choose to die.

Quality was not simply delicious drinks in the middle of the night. His ability to adapt to shrinking horizons stemmed from his own heroic strength, but also from much else which fed that strength and allowed it to flourish.

One element was certainly being at home - the home we had created together, on which he had lavished such care, in which we had had such happy times together and with friends.

Wonderful though the loving care had been on the ward, there is something enervating and debilitating about being in hospital. However generous the regime, you are not in charge, cannot call the tune, are not on your own territory. We were both clear we wanted him to be cared for at home - and he wanted, as he said, to die on our sofa with his head in my lap.

That the ward staff and the community care team unreservedly understood and accepted this choice of ours put us back in charge and left us to live freely according to our own rhythms.

We were given that degree of control, too, in full participation in planning the immensely complex, constantly changing medical and drugs regime. Opting for quality led to the decision, for example, to start on steroids, with all the possible - but to us both, acceptable - risks, and similarly, constantly, in every respect the costs and benefits of one course of action or another were jointly reviewed and action agreed.

The practical realities - endless, complex, demanding as they were - existed within a rich context of relationships: with doctors, nurses, friends, family and between the two of us.

There was no time at which we ever felt any kind of isolation; indeed there was such a constant outpouring of affection and support from professionals and friends alike that we were buoyed up by it in our storm-tossed sea which could otherwise have been so terrifying and threatening.

Between the two of us there was a degree of peace and intimacy which intensified as the months progressed. We had, over the two years of illness, covered so much ground together - said all that we had to say, looked in the face of death, mourned the progressive loss of strength, faculty, our joint future - that we had nothing to do but to be together, to relish each other's simple continuing existence. This, too, was part of his experience of quality.

Towards the end I was struck by the strange beauty of his unreserved dependence, his vulnerable, child-like helplessness, his confidence, faith. His frailty, his decline from such strong, capable, self-assured adulthood broke my heart, but I was moved by the trust which allowed his needs to be so apparent, so available, so readily expressed. What frightened me was fear of my insufficiency to meet them, to remain patient and kind, and, at times, to keep going at all. He remained concerned about my welfare to the end.

Death had been predicted before - months before - on several occasions. On one such occasion - a Saturday - he had hardly been conscious for three days - I sat with him almost the entire day, holding his hand, preparing myself. In the evening he came round and we talked a little. I asked him if he felt that time was closing in. He asked me if that was what the doctors thought. I said yes and asked him if he was frightened of what lay ahead. No, he said, it was only the process - possible pain - which frightened him. He went back to sleep. I sat and waited, then got into bed beside him, lay listening for a time, and eventually slept for a little while.

Sunday morning, he woke bright and talkative, hungry, humorous, demanding tea and scrambled egg. I was knocked for six, hardly able to respond to positive, chirpy demands from the emotional depth of the death-watch I had been through. He'd done it again! 'Death be not proud!' - he was not going until he was ready - certainly not on the say-so of the doctor - not until the last urge for the smallest pleasure had gone for good - and that was not to be for a further six weeks or so.

We talked together and with the medics about dying, about his needing 'permission' to go, not least from me - with my stubborn, instinctive tendency to hold on, to protect and prolong his precious existence: how could I say 'goodbye' knowing that it might allow him to die?

For him the problem was different: 'What do I have to do?' he asked the consultant in one of their conversations.

'Look through the brochures and decide where you want to go,' was the essence of the profoundly wise and helpful response. I don't know if that's what he did, but what I know is that he let go when quality went, and that was, not coincidentally, at the time I felt it had gone too.

The day before he died - he was barely conscious - was a day of mess and discomfort and urgent practical demands. Early in the day there were three or four of the medical team in the house, including the registrar who had suggested she would insert a urine catheter (he had not up to that day been incontinent).

I took her aside and said that I felt the last vestige of quality had now gone, and that he would no longer wish to be kept going (the catheter was a powerful symbol of all that he had wanted to avoid - indignity, loss of control especially). I also said how aware I was that such a judgement risked reflecting my own needs rather than his, but even so I felt I knew his mind. I showed her the paragraph from the Euthanasia Society's *Living Will* which we had both included in our wills ('If there is no reasonable prospect of my recovery...I request that I be allowed to die...and that I receive whatever quantity of drugs may be required to keep me free from pain or distress even if the moment of death is hastened.') 'What do you want me to do?' she asked. 'Nothing,' I replied (quite unable to take responsibility for making a request which, in any case, I knew she could not fulfil), 'but don't do anything that will prolong it.'

After two or three hours, everything was in order - after days of coughing, his throat had cleared, the catheter was in, there was clean bed-linen, he was comfortable and asleep. I felt a great sense of relief - as if some physical and emotional mountain had been climbed, and there was a peaceful, clear view to the horizon.

I now know that we had both let go. And that night he died.

I was much less troubled by the moment of death and by his body than I had imagined. The nurse who was sitting in that night laid him out and went home, leaving me alone in the house. I felt a kind of affectionate familiarity about the body, but its power was only in what it reminded me of and the loss of that made me cry. But it was not in any sense him lying there, it was merely a discarded shell.

So, when they came later to take 'him' away - after his mum and family had arrived to sit by the bed for a while - I did not feel that I was being dispossessed, that he was being taken from me; a potent symbol yes, and the wrench was detaching myself from its meaning not its substance, for he had gone forever in the night, hours before.

We took leave of him at an emotional and extravagant funeral at the London Lighthouse: we had discussed it last autumn with the friend who was to be master of ceremonies on the day, and we knew it was to be a party. 'A leave-taking and a celebration of his life and courage' - with music chosen by him, with friends and family sharing their memories of him with tears, much laughter - and an inordinate amount of champagne.

It was a moving and wonderful occasion - with time and opportunity for companionable grief before and after the non-religious ceremony; with those who had had so much pleasure in his company leaning with their champagne on his coffin as if it were on a bar, talking, reminiscing, laughing, crying.

For me it created such a vivid, rich picture of his thirty-two years that I felt him restored to me in his full vigour - moving the diminished, suffering patient into a less overwhelming perspective, placing it in the context of a whole life, full of energy, humour and pleasure. It was a grand finale which, to my surprise, left me strengthened and comforted, with a sense of fulfilment rather than of bereavement.

I have felt, too, that my burden of grief has been less than I expected: we cried and mourned together a good deal over the last two years - mourned the progressive loss of strength, energy, opportunity; cried as we reconciled ourselves to the fact that the companionable old age we had envisaged would not occur. But we had also been deeply satisfied with - proud of - what we had achieved together over nearly nine years, and especially how in the two years since he had become ill we had done all we could and had left so little unfinished business between us.

So, the house is empty, and I, bereft of the centre and anchor of my life. But he is still here, within me - not in any bizarre psychic sense - but inasmuch as the fruits of living, sharing, learning, growing in the sweetness of intimacy can never be taken away. Being single again is a miserable fact of life in the short term, but I face it with an enduring sense of fulfilment, of pride in what we made together of the hazardous enterprise of being human; and - like him - I face the future with a determination to find quality, not in reminiscence or nostalgia, not in idle aching for the unattainable, but in the best that is possible now, at this very moment.

EPILOGUE
by
Rob George and Vicky Robinson

We earn our living looking after the incurably ill and dying, in what is called Specialist Palliative Care. It is an occupation considered by some - including most of our clinical colleagues - as bizarre or even perverse. Yet, for us, it is an inestimable and most humbling privilege.

We spend our time with people facing the unwanted and uncomfortable. The ragged edge, where every experience is interpretable as a suffering or an opportunity and where the uncertainties may become the ingredients of conquests. However, the intimate details are seldom known to professional intruders such as us. We come, say a few things, and go. The hours and days of attrition go unmarked. We are inclined to see our brief encounters as the fulcrum of a family's day (Bruce and Roy were a family). It is only when we see behind the curtain of their universe that it is so clear how peripheral and on occasion inappropriate our actions were.

Every death is unique. To say that one is better than another would be ludicrous, but Roy's and Bruce's story gives us an opportunity to put our thanks and a few thoughts in print. They represent, if you like, a type: a death in which there was much life, and a separation which, by its coming, led a relationship to deepen probably beyond what it would otherwise have been. In other words a good death: one in which tasks were fulfilled, relationships resolved and meaning found despite the meaninglessness of a young life lost.

We would like to say three things: first, this book stands in its own right. It is the journal of a relationship that is self-validating, but has needed to be formalised, as much as anything because the process has helped Bruce to make sense. In that process, we also have the opportunity to reflect and make sense. That is the challenge to each reader. What an encouragement to each of us as fellow travellers to experience the humour as well as the pain of Roy's passing. We also see that quality is indeed a changeable thing and that the true span of a moment is determined by what is done with it - half the narrative is devoted to the last days of Roy's life.

Secondly, as professionals, this account is remarkable in that it confirms so much for us. It shows all the things that we say and teach: dying is a process, not an event; letting go may take weeks or months, but remains very much in the hands of the patient; time is an elastic thing (compare the pace of the accounts about the world trip with the hours around the death) and so on. What is clear to us at least, is that we have no place attempting to manipulate that process - no matter what we do, someone dies when they die and takes the time they need and that's it. Our job is to create the decision space and the encouragement to take risks, and to wring every last drop from the time that runs through the fingers.

Finally, thank you, Bruce, for keeping diaries, for putting them in print and most of all for having permitted us to contribute in some small way to Roy's care.

Dr. Rob George was Roy's Community Palliative Care Consultant. Vicky Robinson was one of the Palliative Team's Community Care Nurses.

Pentamadine
Drug used for the treatment of PCP (see above)

Steroids
Drugs offering short-term quality of life, but in the long-term could cause problems or shorten life by causing vulnerabilty to infections.

* * *

The Last Word
Cause of Roy's death as recorded
in the hospital autopsy report:
*Acute sphenoid sinusitis and
osteomyelitis of sphenoid bone;*
AIDS.

29/4
bank Hol
weekend.

Time continu
last wrote -
into oblivion!
          Hugh's

agreeable do on a lovely
for the first time & John
years. dad was in hospi
so Mum was doing her du-lit but
          Seen a few film
          Rain Man - o
          ttle Bonfire

20/9 got up early - 9.00ish - set o
akky weather - poped into estate offic
then to kinlochbervie   to fishing port
to Smoo Cave got wet crossing river +
having picnic had a cup of tea with dick
puncture then onto tongue - popped into ham
the newsagent man - no luck. got type
ev,   old times.

31/3 Lynn's leaving d
1+2/4. to bed. Went shop
          luckily going to R
          night sat but u
          nice day - had
          miles to new
          back got back

1/7/90 Sun
          Woke i
          feelings t
          latch onto
          pissed t
          get pissec
          a drin
          so I
          birds
          Sorting
          + fe
          other
          wind
          + r